Contents

Notes on the Authors

Claire Wilcox is Curator of the exhibition *Versace at the V&A*. In 2001, she curated the highly successful V&A exhibition *Radical Fashion* and edited the accompanying book. She is also author of *Bags* (V&A, 1999) and, with Valerie Mendes, *Modern Fashion in Detail* (V&A, 1998).

Valerie Mendes was formerly head of the Department of Textiles and Dress at the V&A. She is a specialist in 20th-century dress and is the author of *Black in Fashion* (V&A, 1999), *Modern Fashion in Detail* (with Claire Wilcox) and *British Textiles 1900-1937* (V&A, 1992)

Chiara Buss is Chief Curator of the Textile Museum at the Antonio Ratti Foundation in Como. She curated an exhibition on the work of Gianni Versace shown in Milan in 1989, and an up-dated version in Como and Miami in 1998-99. She is a specialist in woven textiles and is the author of several publications on Italian Renaissance and 18th-century silks.

Acknowledgments

We would like to express our thanks to Donatella and Santo Versace for their great generosity in making the Gianni Versace archive available to the Museum for the exhibition *Versace at the V&A*, thus making it possible to publish this tribute to their brother, the late Gianni Versace.

Our gratitude also goes to the staff of Gianni Versace S. p. A., in particular Patrizia Cucco and Nadia Conegian for their dedication, hospitality and patience, Enrico Genevois and Jason Weisenfeld. All the clothes and the mannequin and textile photographs have been kindly supplied by, and are the property of, the Archivio Gianni Versace S. p. A.

We would like to express our gratitude to the late Antonio Ratti and the Fondazione Antonio Ratti, Como, Italy, for kindly allowing us to reprint Chiara Buss's text. The material included in the section, 'The Craft of Gianni Versace', first appeared as 'The Reinvention of Materials' in the catalogue to the exhibition, *Gianni Versace La Reinvenzione della Materia* which took place in 1998 at the Fondazione Antonio Ratti. The first version of the text appeared in 1989 in *Un abito per pensare* by Nicoletta Bocca and Chiara Buss.

We are also indebted to the work of the late Richard Martin and Harold Koda of the Costume Institute at the Metropolitan Museum of Art, New York.

Major exhibitions and publications depend on the hard work of many. The following V&A staff have made a particular contribution: The V&A Exhibitions Department: Tessa Hore, Exhibition Co-ordinator, Mike Malham, Exhibition Designer, Paul Stewart, Graphic Designer, Jane Drew and Linda Lloyd Jones; Jane Pavitt and Carlyn Sargentson of the Research Department; Monica Woods, Mary Butler, Clare Davis and Geoff Barlow of V&A Publications; also Marion Kite, Moira Gemmil, Sarah Morris, Debra Isaac, Helen Beeckmans, Rebecca Ward and Damien Whitmore. Special thanks go to Valerie Mendes, formerly Chief Curator of the Department of Textiles and Dress at the V&A for her invaluable contribution.

Thanks are also due to the book designer Kenneth Carroll of Carroll Associates, and editor Rachel Connolly.

We are grateful to the Friends of the V&A for supporting the exhibition.

Published to coincide with the opening of the exhibition 'Versace at the V&A', this book celebrates the work of Gianni Versace (1946–1997), one of the most colourful and talented designers of the late twentieth century.

The house of Versace is not associated with the timid wearer. Versace was famous for dressing the most glamorous of women in his luxurious and high-impact styles. The book features such landmarks as Elizabeth Hurley's infamous safety-pin dress, an evening dress worn by Princess Diana, and clothes made for celebrities from the music industry, such as Elton John, Madonna and Courtney Love.

Versace was a man of inexhaustible energy and enthusiasm. He delighted in all forms of creativity and loved museums, including the V&A. His passion for contemporary and historical art is reflected by sections devoted to work inspired by 'art' and 'history'. Versace found another stage for his talent in opera and ballet productions, and the book features some of these stunning theatrical pieces. Other sections are devoted to jewelled and embroidered couture garments, classical eveningwear, leather creations, tailoring and printed fabrics, illustrating the diversity of Versace's work over three decades. These are discussed by Valerie Mendes in 'The Art of Gianni Versace'.

Chiara Buss investigates a less familiar aspect to the designer in the final section, 'The Craft of Gianni Versace', for he was greatly intrigued by the possibilities of materials, and developed revolutionary ways of treating fabric. Close-up images of many of these technological triumphs are provided, such as the metal 'Oroton' mesh which Versace developed early in his career, continuing to exploit its possibilities until his last collection.

Versace remains one of the leading fashion houses in the world. Based in Milan in a magnificent Italian palazzo, it is still a family-run business. Since 1997, Donatella Versace has been the creative director and, as a postscript, the book features several dresses from her recent collections.

The Art of Gianni Versace

The Art of Gianni Versace by Valerie Mendes

Gianni Versace's first ever presentation in a museum took place on 2 October 1985 in the Victoria and Albert Museum among Raphael's sixteenth-century tapestry cartoons. It was a perfect venue for his work, in which elements from the past were intertwined (often iconoclastically) with the present to inform the future. A museum environment was clearly a second home to Versace. As his team finalized arrangements in the V&A, his excited response to and keen analysis of surrounding historical artefacts was infectious. Though the gala celebrated Gianni Versace, top international designer and show man, his address the following day in a lecture theatre overflowing with young students permitted a rare insight into Versace the consummate professional in his reserved, behind-the-scenes persona. He emphasized the serious value of training, experience and hard work, outlining the critical processes that underpinned every collection. Not easy to please, the student audience was won over by his obvious dedication, generosity (answering a barrage of questions) and quiet charm. The museum/designer collaboration took place at a key point in Versace's career – just seven years after he had launched his own label and twelve years before the tragedy of his murder. The V&A event threw light on the forces that motivated him but, most significantly, indicated the main direction his creative drive was to take. Replete with subtexts and references, his subsequent collections were to become ever more glamorous, provocative and sexually charged. While they shocked and alienated a minority, they attracted and delighted a world-wide clientele, invariably fuelling critical debate.

From various perspectives, monographs, exhibition catalogues and countless reviews and profiles have scrutinized Versace's personal life and output. They chart his early career in detail – the apprenticeship in his mother's dressmaking establishment in Reggio di Calabria, his move north to Milan in 1972 as a ready-to-wear designer for the likes of Genny, Complice and Callaghan, and his first independent collection of 1978. Versace's prêt-à-porter designs were always distinctive but had to comply with the demands of a middle market, avoiding outré statements that were later central to his own label. By the late 1970s, Milan was a firm fixture (for buyers and press alike) on the international fashion circuit and Italy's garment industry was booming. Its infrastructure included luxury textile manufacturers and a multiplicity of specialized ateliers making fine accessories by hand in a range of materials, especially leather. Versace flourished in this milieu, establishing an enduring network of suppliers and creative talents. The tradition of family-operated businesses remained strong in Italy – the Ferragamo, Missoni and Fendi dynasties ensuring the formula proved a resounding success in fashion's domain. Versace maintained this practice, co-opting the business talents of his brother Santo, the design skills of his sister and muse Donatella, and the fashion experience of her husband Paul Beck. It proved a formidable combination that transformed a single shop in Milan into an international company controlling almost 300 outlets and a nine-figure turnover. As the empire grew, diverse profit-making lines were added to the fashion collections, from perfumes to luxury furnishings, with some Versace goods being produced outside the company under lucrative licensing arrangements.

Versace's designs were never for the fainthearted – from the outset his collections made powerful statements, winning acclaim for their assurance and versatility. His restless eclectic imagination roamed a wide spectrum for inspiration. In the early 1980s he gave the English country look a new dynamic with variations on tweed jackets, jodhpurs and chunky cord suits for men and women; for Spring–Summer 1981 he presented softly draped styles based on untailored clothes from the sub-continent, while the next season saw his first 'B-movie' interpretations of Graeco-Roman costume. For the company's advertising campaigns leading photographer Richard Avedon captured successive collections with innovative panoramas of sultry male and female mannequins, their sprawling bodies interlocked as if caught mid-bacchanal. Much imitated, these images marked the start of a long and productive liaison. As Versace began to investigate the far reaches of sexuality and fashion, so Avedon kept pace with undeniably erotic group photographs that set naked bodies against fully-clothed models. Though commercial ventures, Versace relished these commissions for the opportunity to work with a great photographer and make an impact in the realm of advertising. Similarly he collaborated with other eminent photographers including Bruce Weber, who took compelling shots (many in graphic black and white) of Versace menswear. While highlighting the clothes they also represented homoerotic testaments to the virility and physical beauty of young male models.

By the mid-1980s, Versace was internationally renowned for ultra-glamorous eveningwear – the hub of his operation and key to its success. High-profile glamour attracted the world's glitterati and its attendant razzmatazz. Versace showstoppers gratified everyone – celebrities won the attention they craved, the press got good copy plus strong, sexually loaded images, and Versace received excellent publicity. All aspects of the company's marketing strategy were carefully orchestrated – full page adverts in glossy magazines, interviews with Versace, the aggrandizing volumes (*Versace Signatures*, *Men Without Ties*, etc.), and, at collection time, front row seats for 'A list' beautiful people. At considerable cost he hired mega-models for catwalk shows and dressed film stars, pop musicians and a host of other celebrities in camera-ready, body-conscious creations for appearances at glitzy events, be it a film premiere, the Oscars or the Cannes Film Festival. The label was popularly associated with a supermodel fraternity embracing Christy Turlington, Naomi Campbell, Linda Evangelista, Cindy Crawford, Claudia Schiffer, Jerry Hall and Helena Christensen. And when it was time to flaunt themselves in front of the paparazzi, a flattering Versace gown that made the most of voluptuous curves was an obvious choice for the well-toned Elizabeth Hurley, Madonna, Courtney Love and, most prestigiously, Princess Diana.

Versace's concentration on eveningwear resulted in a fast-moving sequence of looks. Delving into fashion history, he borrowed from the distant past but also reworked styles perfected by twentieth-century couturiers he most admired. Thus he paid homage to Madame Grès and Madeleine Vionnet in bias-cut, draped gowns. Though evocative of the 1930s in ivory and pastel-coloured silks, they were totally Versace in their late twentieth-century open sensuality, utilizing techniques (boning and fastening) that would have thoroughly alarmed the two grandes dames. He acknowledged the creativity of Paul Poiret in evening

gowns with extraordinary, swelling, gourd-like skirts, while the master Cristobal Balenciaga was honoured in black lace dresses with flirtatious bows in pale blue and pink. Neat, vivacious tailor-mades referred to Chanel's famous suits, Versace making his hand apparent in extra short skirts and choice of fabrics – an assortment of sugar almond coloured synthetic bouclés (Autumn–Winter 1994–95) and a 'torn' Prince of Wales checked worsted (Spring–Summer 1994).

That classic evening garment – the figure-hugging sheath – was regularly subjected to Versace interpretations. Often in plain black, his risqué designs (long and short) revealed as much as they concealed, featuring deeply carved out necklines and skirts slashed to the thigh. Versace employed a favourite ploy of the two-in-one dress, combining a virtuous covered-up look with vampish cut-outs and slits. Occasionally, insets of beaded openwork allowed titillating glimpses of nubile flesh. All restraint was abandoned in a group of dazzlingly patterned sheath gowns. He used silk printed in loud colours with Andy Warhol-inspired Marilyn Monroe and James Dean portraits for a tight, floor-length creation (1991). Print alone did not suffice; Versace had the bodice decorated with appliqué and multicoloured beads in a device he often returned to: a whorled 'breast plate'. Linda Evangelista wore the gown with sparkling cuff bracelets that almost reached her elbows, and matching handbag with impracticably ornate beaded handles. In similar vein, a silk-screen printed with *Vogue* covers made an evening sheath with a lavishly embroidered halter neck. Most of these creations had inner foundations to give support, shape and a degree of security.

Achieving maximum drama in the mid-1990s, skin-tight minimalist columnar dresses were confined to bold, plain colours, their striking simplicity relieved only by scalloped or asymmetrical necklines, geometric cut-outs and dangerously low, hollowed out arm holes. Versace's particular brand of 'second skin' bodysuits were even more tantalizing than the sheath gowns. The most adventurous coincided with a period in which Versace, a skilled colourist, ran amok with a vivid palette. In 1990 he outdid Pucci in Lycra catsuits printed in clashing, gaudy colours with a dissonant patchwork of Baroque ornament, neo-classical busts, gold-coloured chains, fans, inscriptions and abstract motifs. A year later he went an extravagant stage further with stretch catsuits embroidered all over with polychromatic glistening beads and silks.

Like his contemporaries, Versace was intrigued by the notion of underwear surfacing as outerwear. Advocating a soft mood, he frequently experimented with a sensual feminine style based on the classic, slightly flared, princess-line petticoat with narrow straps, low V-neck and lace trimming. Remaining faithful to the insubstantial slip dress, he rang the changes by teaming metal mesh or transparent tulle with fragile laces and embroidery. Deconstructing the format in the mid-1990s to give it a sexually explicit, wicked gloss, he introduced permanently crumpled satin, skirts side slit to hip level and wide shoulder straps fastened with punk-related gilt kilt pins. In 1996 a series of contour-clinging stretch jersey slips appropriated features from seductive satin petticoats, while their streamlined nature was enhanced by brightly coloured inset tapering lines echoing the speed lines of professional sportswear. Versace was well aware of fetishist obsessions and the clandestine allure of tightly laced stays when he quoted from eighteenth- and nineteenth-century corsetry in cream, baby blue and pink full-length evening gowns. Their top-stitched bodices and inlaid panels echoed the parallel lines of historical boning. It was only a short step from this faux innocence to the more sinister, black garments of 1992–93 that took their lead from a sado-masochistic underworld. Some felt that this time Versace had gone too far, forgetting that (like it or not) there were few if any limits in post-modern fashion with its 'anything goes' attitude.

Critic-friendly, lyrical gowns illustrated a different, less threatening fantasy as well as Versace's skill with difficult-to-handle filmy materials such as chiffon and georgette, which he cut to glide over slender bodies in sensuous layers. Like so much of his work they demonstrated Versace's preoccupation with the fine and applied arts. Patterns to suit each slimline gown were adapted from a wide decorative repertoire – Minoan ceramics, Graeco-Roman ornament, Art Deco and contemporary art movements; Versace dipped and mixed without hesitation, drawing on his extensive library and diverse art collection.

That long-established convention, the opulent ballgown of fitted bodice, nipped-in waist and ballooning skirt, did not escape his attention. Between 1994 and 1995 Versace's fairytale ballgowns had billowing skirts arranged asymmetrically in copious irregular pleats and drapes over similarly treated underskirts. Sun ray pleats and scattered embroidered flowers added texture and a feminine aura. Though influenced by eighteenth- and nineteenth-century precedents, Versace brought his creations up to the minute with backless bodices held together by chunky elastic 'braces', while long, straight pins stuck through the frothy skirts of a black and white gown made dual reference to the functional straight pins that fastened eighteenth-century dress and the symbolically aggressive pins of punk. Other ballgown variants were separates of tight, richly embroidered bodice tops and immensely bouffant skirts, their asymmetrical volume achieved by intricate layers held aloft on stiffened petticoats.

Above all, Versace was devoted to Oroton, his patented metallic 'material' first shown in 1982. Enthusiasm for metal mesh never waned; each season new evening styles emerged – long or short, draped or straight cut. Remaining oblivious to its disadvantages (it snagged easily, was cold and could be exceedingly heavy), he had it coloured, encrusted with diamantés and married to other fabrics. At its most successful it caressed the body in revealing, subtly draped garments that exploited the appeal of gold and silver glinting against bare skin. Taking advantage of the fact that such gowns were usually the centre of attention, Versace created wedding dresses for sirens in glistening Oroton. His last collection (Autumn–Winter 1997–98) starred a double-layered mini bridal gown of silver metal mesh adorned with glittering Greek crosses; worn by Naomi Campbell, it was the climax of the show.

Eveningwear even invaded daywear in 'poor little rich girl', night/day ensembles that paired luxurious silks with blue denim 'workwear'. Long, layered, multipatterned silk skirts (inspired by eighteenth-century modes) had unexpected companions of sturdy-looking indigo denim shirts, while gold embroidered silk moiré jackets over matching bustiers were worn with casual denim jeans.

Though overshadowed by high-profile evening collections, Versace daywear epitomized clean-cut Milanese chic, exhibiting the designer at his most discreet. Immaculately made, short-skirted suits were bought by women executives wishing to place an emphasis on femininity yet convey power and efficiency in the workplace. Versace perfected asymmetrical tailoring long before it became widespread on the world's catwalks, and injected a fresh vitality into classics such as the trench coat and two-piece city suit. He built on his experience in ready-to-wear but, as his own master, was free to make occasional discordant flourishes. Thus he composed a hound's tooth checked coat with a collar so high that it almost obliterated the head, and fastened a sleek pin-striped jacket with a giant floppy bow in a loud flowery print. For autumn and winter, expensive, lightweight wools and fine napa leather meant that garments were warm but never overly heavy. Smart black, white and grey enlivened with touches of red enhanced sharp silhouettes and were favoured for cold weather designs. The same intense red recurred in tailored asymmetrical jackets, coats and streamlined day dresses with innovative pod-shaped skirts. Memorable summer inventions included primary coloured Bermuda outfits in crisp cotton with pleated shorts inspired by Balinese costume, while stark, rectangular linen shifts had front panels looped to the waist at one side, the loop emphasized by a single bold stripe. Versace was fascinated by the visual impact of layering and pleating and related processes; typically he was interested in pleats and layers as dominant factors rather than occasional decorative notes. Technical investigations resulted in extraordinary garments ranging from skirts composed of horizontal rows of minute flounces ordered with mathematical precision to entire rippled dresses of deep, irregularly pleated tiers.

As he had done with his womenswear collections, in 1979 Versace brought his adventurous spirit to menswear, breaking many creatively stifling conventions in clothes that were notable for their panache and glamour. Together with Armani in the mid-1980s he deformalized the suit, introducing big-shouldered, loose-fitting jackets and generously cut trousers. For summer they engineered a minor revolution with cool, pure linen suits in muted neutral colours that were instantly copied for high street consumption. Dishevelled linen was soon an untidy but internationally accepted mode; to maximize the look Versace commissioned linen with a permanently crumpled finish. For almost twenty years he supplied men of means and daring with out-of-the-ordinary clothes. Throughout his career he explored alternatives to commonplace trousers, trawling global styles for ideas to adapt. Trouser pleats were transformed into panels that extended down the leg, draped constructions such as the dhoti and panung proved inspirational, and wrapover skirts for men stimulated press coverage. For formal apparel he tried novel structures and added eye-catching gilt details.

Wide-shouldered, square-cut jackets gave way to the slender, long-line tailoring of Versace's last collections. Though he worked with the 'safe' navy, brown, black or grey ranges of plain, checked and striped worsteds, he also offered venturesome textured and figured weaves in colours traditionally restricted to womenswear. Evening and casual collections offered him the artistic licence he cherished; the outcome attracted extroverts and risk takers, and celebrity clients included Elton John, Prince, Sylvester Stallone and Bruce

Springsteen. Evening unorthodoxy put leather trousers or jeans with extra long, brightly coloured or heavily embroidered waistcoats and elegant tailcoats. The latter were superbly tailored but defied Savile Row canons with 'cowboy' gilt-tipped collars, insignia Medusa-head buttons and square-cut tails; Sting chose one for his marriage to Trudie Styler in 1992. Linen remained in Versace's repertoire for most summers – in 1989 he received due praise for printed-to-shape garments for men and women. Of particular note in navy and cream, men's suits had crossover, triangular fronted, printed waistcoats and jackets with exceptionally narrow, printed revers. Bruce Weber photographed their overt dandyism, modelled appropriately by mannequins masquerading as new-wave teddy boys. The tight fit of Versace jeans appealed to exhibitionists as did his over-the-top reworking of Hawaiian shirts, printed in garish colours in an assortment of kitsch designs. Without inhibition Versace emblazoned men's shirts and – more alarmingly – jeans with bold prints. It was hardly surprising to spot an 'in your face' black and white 1992 outfit (copy or otherwise) looking of-the-moment and strutting the streets at Trinidad's body-conscious Carnival, 2002.

Versace pushed materials to their very limits; though he expected a lot from them, in return he endowed them with new identities. Like metal mesh, leather was not exempt – he had it embroidered, studded, pleated, crumpled, embossed and gilded. Collection after collection included leather for men and women, with black being the preferred 'colour'. Ever preoccupied with the ramifications of the black leather jacket he produced numerous variations – some were unisex, others obtained male or female identities via cut and detailing. Addicted to biker jackets, he made a speciality of the studded blouson. In 1991 Peter Lindberg photographed a line-up of petulant supermodels in Versace leathers, pleated mini skirts and clumpy boots; in deference to their stylistic source they wore caps à la Marlon Brando in *The Wild One* (1954). Men could be clad entirely in Versace body-skimming, tailored leathers enlivened with jacket panels, and trousers covered in minute glittering studs. Evening dresses frequently came with sophisticated lightweight leather jackets. Notorious 1990s versions embroidered with large crosses were worn over halter tops with bejewelled representations of the Madonna and vilified as sacrilegious. Simply cut black napa mini dresses enjoyed focus points of sparkling Greek crosses or Japanese symbols and calligraphy. Manipulating leather as if it were pliable silk, Versace cajoled it into complex structures, the most ambitious being padded and quilted coats with fitted long-sleeved tops and flared skirts. Resembling soft sculptures, they harked back to Charles James' pneumatic, down-filled evening jacket of 1937.

As a theatrical costumier Versace was in his element, and the world of performance wholeheartedly welcomed his uninhibited exuberance. After designs for Strauss ballets at La Scala in 1982 and 1983, he began a lifetime's collaboration with choreographer Maurice Béjart. Henceforward a symbiotic relationship developed between Versace's high fashion and stage (mainly ballet and opera) costumes – a happy state of cross-fertil-ization with some impressive outcomes. Vibrant dance costumes for *Java For Ever* had fashion counterparts in sophisticated evening gowns with black tulle backgrounds embroidered in vivid silks and glittering beads, with abstract devices, circus acrobats and horses interspersed with cosmological images. Among his most sensational pieces were huge and commanding operatic costumes based on Victorian crinolines. Each component was larger than life and gigantic skirts were ornamented with striking patterns in appliqué, quilting and cordwork. Renaissance and eighteenth-century fashions were plundered for fanciful, exuberant male costumes.

Versace employed his ability as a colourist to create arresting multicoloured as well as monochromatic costumes. Capable of subdued moments, for Béjart's dance *Souvenir de Leningrad* he designed cream on cream with touches of silver tutus: refined exercises in texture achieved by skilful cutwork embroidery, pin tucks and scallops. With short bouffant skirts and a *jeune fille* aura, tutus were translated for the catwalk into sprightly dresses with tight bodices and very short bell skirts over hooped petticoats. Smooth silk tiers, each printed with a different brightly coloured, small-scale floral pattern (based on Russian textiles), emphasized their innocence in complete contrast to the 'adults only' sexuality implicit in much of Versace's output.

A retrospective inevitably highlights a handful of works that for one reason or another are deemed to be showstoppers or milestones. The media furore over 'that dress' worn by Elizabeth Hurley when she accompanied Hugh Grant to the London premiere of *Four Weddings and a Funeral* (May 1994) ensured that the name Versace will always be associated with sexy black dresses. Now an icon in the evolution of the little black dress, there can be no doubt that its celebrity-linked lasciviousness will be revisited by the press and live on in fashion histories. Similarly, the gold-studded, sky blue gown worn by Princess Diana in 1992 was endowed with intimate meaning that exceeded its significance as an exquisite evening dress. It moved to another plane, attaining from Princess Diana a magnetic appeal that will forever evoke her beauty and elegance. Other works are no less resonant as they define key moments and elements in Versace's oeuvre. A sensuous sheath of 1992 betrays the designer's devotion to florid ornament – gilded eighteenth-century curlicues and printed fanciful, large-scale interpretations of animal skins and furs were particular favourites. Superimposing one on the other he demonstrated his ability to compel apparently discordant parts into a successful harmony. Part of his strategy to surprise and shock, a dominatrix-inspired gown showed how he transcended the restricted culture of S+M to create a complex example of haute couture out of leather straps and silk. A golden pillar of a gown in Versace's unique metal mesh signifies his career-long desire to flatter the female body and transform women into shining heroines.

Versace fashioned himself into the master of conspicuous consumption, choosing not to make understatement his métier. Taking full advantage of a market niche that existed for his type of sophisticated excess, he set the pace in terms of fashion daring and insolence. He courted controversy and it came in accusations of vulgarity and brashness which in fact played into his schema. As a multitalented designer he was able to counter the extremes of his most bizarre 'Hollywood' extravaganzas with outstanding, pared down designs of unadorned simplicity. A polymath, he culled ignition points for his designs from the fine and applied arts, fashion history, street styles and popular culture, resulting in a kaleidoscopic pageant of fashion. It was often bewildering in its eclecticism, but the guiding constants were superb technique and Versace's singular vision.

Showstoppers

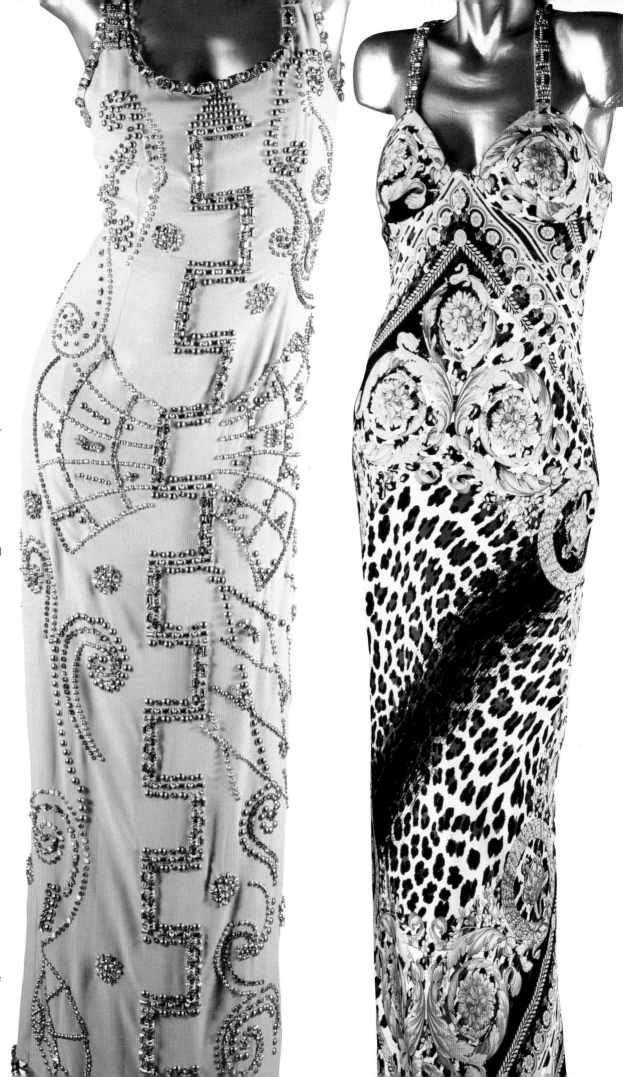

1

Autumn/Winter 1991–92
Evening gown worn by Diana, Princess of Wales. Powder blue reversed satin (matt side uppermost) with gold-tone studs, coloured stones and diamantés.

Throughout the 1990s the Princess of Wales developed a new assurance and sophistication; these worldly attributes were reflected in her taste for body-conscious evening gowns and chic, streamlined daywear. She increasingly wore Versace designs and especially liked his columnar dresses that were ideal for her tall, svelte physique. For the photographic session featuring this gown, her favourite hairdresser Sam McKnight gave the Princess a boyish, slightly tousled haircut and photographer Patrick Demarchelier captured a smiling, lightly tanned Diana, radiant with good health. The gown has a simple shape but the pattern is boldly geometric, with linear whorls and a dominant 'bow' motif that defined the hips. The classical mixture of pale blue and gold perfectly complemented the Princess's blonde and blue-eyed colouring.

2

Autumn/Winter 1991–92
Evening gown. Brown, white and gold printed silk twill with beaded straps.

Versace made the most unlikely pattern combinations succeed. A bias-cut sheath dress has precise seaming in order to match up the pattern, and is composed of a giant, scarf-like panel of leopard print bordered with his favourite 'Wild Baroque' design of foliate volutes and architectonic roundels. Versace was devoted to this pattern evocative of the luxurious past, though he often brought it bang up-to-date in a manner that was astounding and less than reverential. The sensuous mixture of animal skin with regal golden ornament suited his schema, and in a typically impudent move a pair of large, leafy whorls enclosing central floral devices were placed over the breasts. (See Craft 16, p. 137)

3

Autumn/Winter 1992–93
Evening gown. Black acetate
and viscose, black leather, gilt
buckles with amber stones.

By carefully reworking the
components of a conventional
black evening gown Versace
created a powerful garment with
dominatrix overtones, which, at
its launch, caused something of
a furore. Above the waist Versace
composed a bodice featuring
black lace mesh with black
chenille in a beaded cross
pattern. Top-stitched straps,
alternately leather and fabric,
echo the type of attire favoured
by bondage devotees. Versace
deliberately fuelled the
controversy by merging these
taboo elements with the couture
convention of a sheath skirt.

4

Spring/Summer 1994

Evening gown. Black viscose (60%) and acetate (40%) with kilt pin embellishments.

Brimming with associations, this now notorious black dress made headline news when worn by Elizabeth Hurley at the premiere of *Four Weddings and a Funeral*. It revealed almost as much flesh as it concealed and celebrated the voluptuous curves of a well-toned, womanly body. Carefully constructed to stay in place, the V-neck and open sides are boned and the bust is lightly padded. Versace revisited elements from 1970s and 1980s style to achieve this ultimate in seductive attire. It is a distant relative of the black, slashed and safety-pinned clothing of British punk and of the body-conscious black Lycra sheath dresses of metropolitan disco and club life. While he accommodated the principle of anti-establishment slashed clothing, there was nothing untidy or raw-edged about this dress, and mundane safety pins became gilt and silver kilt pins resplendent with diamantés as well as Versace's Medusa-head emblem. The designer put his unique stamp of glamour and audacity on this design, which has become a landmark in the history of the little black dress.

5

Autumn/Winter 1997–98

Evening gown. Gold-tone Oroton with applied beadwork.

Always faithful to and excited by the remarkable metal mesh he had been instrumental in developing in the early 1980s, Versace used it for this gown, apparently unconcerned about the burden of its considerable weight. He kept the cut of the long sheath simple to allow the textures and reflections of the Oroton and beaded Greek crosses to triumph. Over a supporting corselette, the narrow gown is wraparound to permit movement and the cowl neck is boned to keep its shape. Of all his works in shimmering Oroton it takes the popular image of crusading knights in their protective gleaming chain mail into another dimension.

Print

1

Spring/Summer 1993
Shirt. Printed silk.

The Hawaiian shirt provided a
model for Versace's famously
exuberant series of men's leisure
shirts. He used them as
'notebooks' to make graphic
explorations of recurrent themes,
such as characters from popular
culture and motifs culled from
historical patterns. Each vibrantly
coloured shirt has the distinctively
strong, unmistakable Versace
hallmark. In this case, he
juxtaposed images of North
American Indians with Baroque
roundels and flourishes.

2

Spring/Summer 1994
Mini dress. Multicoloured
printed silk georgette.

Though tiny, this garment (an
ultra-sophisticated smock) is
packed with many components. It
has a conventional high shirt
collar attached to very narrow,
multiple rouleau straps above a
smocked and beaded high-
waisted bodice; the beading forms
tiny flowers. The almost
fluorescent palette and fearless
mixture of stripes and bold roses
see Versace in light-hearted,
youthful mode.

3

Spring/Summer 1993
Jumpsuit. Multicoloured
printed silk georgette.

An extravagant amount of
vividly coloured, double-layered
georgette makes a show-
stopping, all-in-one, carnival-like
garment that was paraded on the
catwalk by supermodel Naomi
Campbell. The abstract 'brushy'
print incorporates Medusa
heads. A floating dress (short at
the front, long at the back)
flutters over immensely flared
trousers from a high-waisted
bodice with bright yellow, orange
and blue top-stitched straps
which encircle the breasts.

4

Autumn/Winter 1991–92
Day ensemble, shirt and skirt.
Black and gold printed silk twill.

Versace enjoyed the grandeur and
opulence of architectonic
Baroque patterns printed in gold
and black on white. With panache
and in defiance of tradition he
used these furnishing scale
repeats to adorn an array of
garments as well as accessories
and ceramics. In rule-breaking
mode he set this powerful design
on its side in both the tailored shirt
and the short pleated skirt. So
devoted was Versace to this type
of occasionally overpowering
ornament that it became one of
his most important hallmarks.
(See Craft 15, p. 136)

5

Spring/Summer 1992
Man's outfit, shirt and trousers.
Black and white printed silk and
stretch cotton twill.

In daring mood Versace
composed this brash two-piece
that demanded a good body,
courage and exhibitionist
tendencies. Greek fretwork on a
giant scale marched up and down
the legs, making the tight jeans
extraordinary, while a scaled-
down version of the graphic
pattern was repeated over the
shirt. Clients could play it safe with
just the shirt and a pair of plain
jeans; only intrepid souls would
brave the total look.

6

Autumn/Winter 1990–91
Evening ensemble. Silk taffeta
printed with a spotted fur motif,
silk embroidered with pearls,
diamantés, coloured stones
and bugle beads.

Achieving a gloriously bouffant
skirt, Versace manipulated
rustling taffeta in browns and
black into soft pleats set asymmetrically into a deep waistband. The
skirt, with a diagonal front
opening, curves out like a giant
gourd to knee level then tapers to
the ground. Over black taffeta a
swirling printed fur pattern
emphasizes the movement of the
pleats, is stiffened with net to
retain its shape, and is continued
to form the lining. Though a
strapless body with deep, boned
décolletage is lavishly beaded, it
remains a secondary element to
the magnificent skirt.

7

Spring/Summer 1996
Evening ensemble, top and skirt.
Printed stretch silk (80%) and
Elastane (40%), printed satin.

Versace delighted in the potential
of animal skin prints and issued
visual challenges with some
alarming compositions. Sinuous
white lines on the tight, cap-
sleeved top suggest a zebra's
hide, while the flared, trained skirt
has a black and gold pattern
replicating an exotic spotted fur
and is lined with a similar printed
silk. The train begins at the bottom
of the spine and its clean-edged,
flared profile is maintained by the
heavyweight satin and metal
weights set into the hem.

Leather

1

Autumn/Winter 1992–93
Cocktail suit, jacket and trousers. Black stretch silk and black leather with gilt trimmings and studs.

By carefully reworking the components of a classically tailored winter ensemble Versace created a powerful suit influenced by the preferred wear of sado-masochists. He composed a hard-edged, off-the-shoulder jacket featuring a restraining collar and top-stitched leather straps fastened through jewelled buckles. The jacket is intricately shaped and constructed with inlaid panels and top-stitched bands, while the trousers have gold- and silver-finish studs and white top stitching.

2

Autumn/Winter 1991–92
Ensemble, jacket, sleeveless top and skirt. Black kid leather with gold- and silver-tone metal studs, studded silk and pleated silk crêpe.

Versace took the technique of studding to decorative extremes in this outfit. Metal rivets employed in 19th-century workwear as practical reinforcements for pockets and seams were precursors of fashion studs. Their potential was to be exploited by sub-cultures from rockers to punks as well as couturiers. Used in quantity they increase the weight of a garment enormously, but with customary aplomb Versace surmounted this factor, even studding the skirt's delicate pleated silk crêpe.

3

Autumn/Winter 1992–93
Coat. Padded and quilted
black leather trimmed with fox
fur and astrakan.

The technical complications of
using leather as if it were a supple
fabric never deterred Versace, and
he forged ahead turning leather
into extraordinary garments. He
steered clear of the straight lines of
the commonplace 'duvet' coats
that had proliferated after the
1970s in favour of a glamorous
fitted style. The sleeves are quilted
with a traditional diamond trellis,
whereas the bodice and flared skirt
consist of graduated pneumatic,
concentric circles. A deep belt
with characteristic 'glitzy' Versace
gilt embellishments fastens
around the nipped-in waist.
(See Craft 28, p. 145)

4

Spring/Summer 1993
Man's ensemble, jacket and trousers. Black rubber and leather.

Versace gave a black leather blouson a sportive appeal by inserting arcs of incised rubber over the shoulders and by trimming seams with top-stitched leather 'speed line' bands. Ideas were borrowed from performancewear – ski suits, surfers' neoprenes and professional bike racing leathers – and reworked in black for the fashion market. A high stand-up collar and warm sheepskin lining made the jacket an eminently practical garment. Matching rubber trousers (lined with jersey) have lasered grooves running vertically, adding to the streamlined look.
(See Craft 36, p. 148)

5

Spring/Summer 1993
Man's outfit, jacket and trousers. Black leather with gold- and silver-tone studs.

Versace's menswear collections were rarely without luxurious leather garments. Throughout his career he honed his skill with leather, and each carefully constructed reinvention gave him enormous satisfaction. Far removed from its raunchy biker source, this high-fashion blouson has an unusual pair of long, tapered pockets with button-down flaps. Versace toned down the aggressive side of black leather by decorating the elongated pockets, sleeves and tight, tapered trousers with minute studs.

6

Spring/Summer 1993
Man's jacket. Black leather
with fringes and silver-tone
metal beads.

In soft black leather the jacket
has a fly front with zip fastening
and a deep yoke. Versace rings
the changes with gender-defying,
beaded, extra-long leather fringes
that swing from the yoke's edge.
The back is shaped by an
elasticated waist and has a plain
fringe. Part of Versace's long
involvement with the black leather
jacket, it contains references to a
range of menswear, from biker
gear to American Indian
buckskins. Above all, this jacket
offered an urban cowboy style
and represented the type of
'look at me' design that Versace
excelled at and his celebrity
clients found so desirable.

7

Autumn/Winter 1994–95
Man's jacket. Leather, satin.

This warm and practical leather
jacket has a double-breasted
fastening, elasticated waist and
zippered pockets. In a disruption
of the natural qualities of smooth,
unlined leather, the surface is
patterned with permanent
crinkles, imbuing a luxurious
garment with a casual air, one
of Versace's favourite devices.
The hood is lined with grey
satin brocade with Medusa
motifs. (See Craft 30, p. 145)

8

Autumn/Winter 1994–95
Evening gown. Black silk with
polyurethane coating.

This slender, clinging, wet-look
gown has provocative peepholes
punctuated with gilt and black
Medusa-head buttons. Versace
ceaselessly investigated the
potential of a wide range of fabrics
irrespective of their constituents
or market levels: here he had a
costly silk coated to resemble an
inexpensive plastic; while it
emulates a recalcitrant vinyl it
retains the suppleness of silk.
(See Craft 55, p. 159)

9

Autumn/Winter 1994–95
Mini dress. Bright yellow silk
taffeta coated with polyurethane
with gilt buttons.

This zinging yellow mini has
provocative peepholes demanding
a superlatively confident wearer
with perfect deportment and a
well-toned, youthful body. It makes
reference to the sauciest of 1960s
teenage fashions in form, colour
and fabric, though the carefully
composed gentle arcs at shoulders
and midriff are subtleties
belonging to 1990s Versace. Skin
was vitally important – the
minuscule skirt grazes the thighs,
while pairs of bold gilt buttons (big
enough to fasten a hefty jacket)
draw the eye to the cut-outs and
the flesh beneath. (See Craft 55)

10

Spring/Summer 1996
Mini evening dress.
Leather, synthetic tulle, lace,
beads, sequins.

An uncomplicated sleeveless
shift became a 'canvas' for a richly
textured, abstract design. Irregular
blotches of beaded leather
interspersed with bead clusters
adorn the bodice, while flame-like
tendrils of beaded leather leap up
from the hemline. The midriff is
clearly visible through unadorned
tulle, while the encrusted design
preserves the wearer's modesty.
(See Craft 38, p. 149)

Daywear

1

Autumn/Winter 1984–85
Man's jacket, shirt, waistcoat and
trousers ensemble. Bouclé wool,
Shetland wool, flannel, knit, silk.

Always intrigued by the tactile
qualities of fabric, Versace created
a layered outfit that is a subtle
composite of soft tones and
textures. Using only the best-
quality yarns and cloth, this
ensemble comprises a fine bouclé
shirt in shades of beige and grey
worn under a silk-lined waistcoat of
ribbed knit and flannel, gathered
softly at the waist and closing in a
deep cross fastening. The heavy
Shetland wool striped jacket has a
single button fastening and the
flannel trousers are simply cut and
gathered onto the waist. This is
country-inspired leisurewear for
the town dweller and a rare, early
example of Versace's skill with
knitwear and tweeds.

2

Autumn/Winter 1983–84
Suit, jacket and skirt. Black leather,
black and white checked wool.

In 1988 Versace explained why he
was motivated to develop two-in-
one garments such as this tailored
ensemble with its leather and
woollen check duality:
'There is never just one way of
working on an object. At that
moment I was using leather and
men's fabrics. I wanted to make
them into jackets, but when the
moment came to choose, I didn't
want to deny myself the possibility
of simultaneously displaying the
two jackets that I could have
made.' The top-stitched leather
right side fastens to the checked
wool left side with custom-made
silver and brass buttons.

3

Autumn/Winter 1983–84
Man's casual outfit, trousers and
jacket. Black and white wool
tweed, black leather.

Widely-cut trousers tapering to the
ankles were early entrants into
Versace's stylistic repertoire and
here he conducted further
experiments with the shape.
Familiar trouser pleats become
panels extended down the legs to
a few inches above each hem.
They give the roomy trousers
another dimension – to succeed
they required a confident owner
with a tall, lean physique. For
summer they were available
in cotton gaberdine.

4

Autumn/Winter 1984–85
Tailored jacket. Grey wool.

Of complex cut, this jacket
establishes a contrast between a
right front with large lapel and
protruding pocket and a left front
deprived of both lapel and pocket.
Top-stitched edges crisply
delineate the component parts.
Though adventurous in its
asymmetry and play of volumes
and planes, it is executed in ultra-
conservative dark grey wool.
Broad 1980s 'power dressing'
shoulders have matching rounded
profiles and unite the whole.

5

Spring/Summer 1986
Man's two-piece outfit, trousers
and dust coat with belt. Grey
pin-striped, two-tone linen.

An ensemble that is at once smart
and relaxed gives new meaning to
the pin-stripes of city suits.
Versace was instrumental in
starting the revolutionary vogue for
crumpled linen that was
immediately copied by mass
manufacturers for high-street
consumption. He offered clients
comfort and volume in garments
that were generously cut with
broad shoulders (minus pads) and
wide trousers that tapered to the
ankles. The dust coat with belt and
deep-set raglan sleeves gives the
outfit a dashing 'macho' appeal.

6

Autumn/Winter 1986–87
Man's suit, jacket and trousers. Grey and black wool.

The cut of the suit is powerful – the roomy jacket has hefty shoulders and no-nonsense pockets – but its assertiveness is denied by the wool, with its busy, all-over 'feminine' pattern suggesting animal fur: not the customary cloth for a man's two-piece suit. Versace adored the excitement of each season's fabrics and felt that men should not be confined to the safe grey, black and navy of flannels and worsteds.

7

Autumn/Winter 1987–88
Cocktail dress. Bright red silk.

Versace constantly experimented with techniques, pushing them to the extreme to attain his goal. The notion of horizontal tiers of fabric was far from new but Versace revolutionized the ploy to achieve this witty little dress. He threw caution to the wind lapping wide bands of uneven depth over each other irregularly and introducing randomly placed pleats. Both tiers and occasional pleats create shadows that add a further dimension to the layered composition. The self-aware Versace called these explorations 'the game of the wrong pleats'.

8

Autumn/Winter 1988–89
Swing coat and sweater. Woven black and white hound's tooth checked cashmere and wool mix with printed silk velvet, black cashmere.

A classic coat made from many yards of expensive cashmere and wool with that rarest of features, a silk velvet lining. The hard geometry of the black and white woven check is relieved by glimpses of the printed interior, with its Art Deco-inspired pattern incorporating roundels. These alluring, soft-to-the-touch textiles make a comfortingly warm garment the very height of luxury.

9

Autumn/Winter 1988–89
Skirt. Finely checked black and white worsted with twenty-two carefully overlapped waved horizontal flounces.

Autumn/Winter 1988–89
Skirt. Black leather with narrow, top-stitched leather bands applied in horizontal lines from waist to hem.

Autumn/Winter 1988–89
Figured black and white worsted with narrow strips of the same material organized in a closely spaced vertical formation.

Versace was always intrigued by layering and the potential of bands, flounces and strips arranged as multiple parallel elements. His imagination knew no bounds as he patiently investigated the concept. The results were remarkable three-dimensional, tactile pieces, each dependent upon absolutely impeccable workmanship to avoid any suggestion of bulk; tiered or layered clothes demand ultra-slim wearers. One finely flounced skirt had a shell-like appearance, while another with narrow fabric strips arranged vertically looked like the underside of a mushroom.

10

Autumn/Winter 1989–90
Man's three-piece evening ensemble, jacket, waistcoat and trousers. Fine charcoal grisaille wool, white silk.

Demanding a non-conformist owner, this outfit dispenses with the buttoned-up safety and symmetry of a conservative three-piece suit. Masculinity is asserted in the wide-shouldered, boxy jacket, though this is radically softened by the unorthodox lapels that drape from just below shoulder level to the hem – they flank similarly inventive drapery at the front of the non-fastening waistcoat. The final nonchalant touch is made by an open-necked white silk shirt with black buttons.

11

Autumn/Winter 1990–91
Evening coat dress. White ribbed silk.

Conventional tailoring was based upon balance and strictly matching parts, but here Versace composed an asymmetrical, off-the-shoulder garment in which the fronts are of radically different shapes. The right side is draped to an off-centre fastening, while the slightly shorter left side is crisply tailored in a traditional manner. Top stitching echoes the ribbed silk and stiffens broad bands forming collar and cuffs.

12

Autumn/Winter 1992–93
Suit, jacket and skirt. White wool with black leather and gilt trimmings.

The sharply tailored suit has a fitted jacket with a gilt-tipped collar and matching gilt buttons. The crispness of this two-piece owes something to Chanel, whose work Versace much admired. He loved to surprise by juxtaposing conflicting patterns or references to different eras, but he also played around with scale and function. Here he delighted in three dominant black leather straps in the deliberate knowledge that they were over-the-top and gave an ostensibly conventional white suit a threatening note.

13

Spring/Summer 1993
Man's outfit, jacket, T-shirt, waistcoat and trousers. Black, lightweight wool gaberdine with studded black leather, black leather and printed wool.

A classic single-breasted, tailored black jacket is enlivened by a studded, gilt-tipped leather collar and two pairs of pockets with heavy leather flaps embellished with studs and jewelled gilt 'arrowheads'. Buttons (alternately gold and silver gilt) have the raised Medusa-head Versace logo and fasten through impeccably worked leather-bound buttonholes. The all-black outfit is relieved by touches of glinting metal and the sheen of fine leather.

14

Autumn/Winter 1992–93
Coat. Black alpaca with black leather and gilt studs.

A long, princess-line, cold-weather coat has elegant appeal. The dense black of the luxurious alpaca is relieved by deep leather collar, cuffs and pocket flaps enriched with gilt studs. Versace's favourite gold and black 'Wild Baroque' printed silk twill was quilted to provide a cosy lining. (See Craft 44, p. 154)

15

Autumn/Winter 1991–92
Skirt and jacket. Bouclé wool with lurex threads.

A bouclé wool tweed suit saw Versace at his most quietly flattering. With top-stitched leather collar, leather-edged cuffs and facings and large Medusa-head buttons, the detailing and styling evoke Chanel but the delight in texture and technologically advanced material are typical of Versace, for on closer inspection the black bouclé wool proves to be shot through with gold lurex threads.

16

Spring/Summer 1997
Man's 'Nehru' suit, jacket and trousers. Grey pin-stripe wool, viscose and nylon twill.

A slender, long-line, three-button jacket is single-breasted with the narrowest of stand-up 'Nehru' collars. To maximize the streamlined look Versace introduced long darts and avoided any distracting horizontal elements such as top pockets. This style had been popular in the 1960s among the young and trendy. Though Versace gave it new currency it remained the province of young men and has never usurped the traditional city suit.

17

Autumn/Winter 1988–89
Ensemble, tailored jacket, polo neck sweater, trousers.
Red wool crêpe, black cashmere, black wool.

Versace the purist tailor married innovatory design with traditional fabrics and techniques to achieve new classics. Conventional tailoring was based upon balance and strictly matching parts, but Versace composed a jacket in which the right and left fronts were of a radically different shape. The success of this asymmetry, with its off-the-shoulder right side and high-set left side depended upon immaculate cut and construction. To set off its unorthodox irregularity Versace put it over a stark black sweater and trousers.

The Ballgown

1

Atelier Autumn/Winter 1994–95
Ballgown. Eau de Nil silk
taffeta moiré.

As designers before him, such as
Dior and Balmain, Versace was
intrigued by 19th-century styles.
He took his lead from the long,
tight cuirasse bodice of the 1870s
and 1880s when composing this
exquisite, pastel-coloured
ballgown. Immaculate top-
stitched and corded triangular
panels shape the taffeta and give
the corset-like bodice rigidity.
Each panel terminates at hip level
in a pretty bow. The full, rustling
skirt is supported by a
multilayered petticoat. This formal
and romantic masterpiece – fit for
a debutante – is an eloquent
expression of Versace's haute
couture skills.

2

Atelier Spring/Summer 1994
Ballgown. Charcoal grey pleated
synthetic organza and white silk
shot with lurex.

Versace applied his favourite ruse
of the 'two-in-one dress' to the
ballgown concept, gaining high
effect from an asymmetrical
interplay of black and white. He
skilfully deconstructed the
familiar ballgown format by using
masses of airy organza apparently
swathed at random over sparkly
silk and stuck through with punk-
inspired, large decorative pins. He
achieved volume (supported by a
layered net petticoat) with the
lightest of touch and delighted in
the highly tactile appeal of the
costly materials. Again, and
somewhat mischievously, he kept
the bodice aloft with substantial
'braces' that cross at the back.

3

Atelier Spring/Summer 1994
Ballgown. Pale grey silk and metal georgette, cotton tulle and lurex, jacquard lurex georgette.

Recalling the magnificence and romance of 19th-century ballgowns, with their full skirts and shimmering luxurious fabrics, this gown fuses subtle colour harmony with sumptuous appeal. Emulating a technique favoured by theatrical costumiers, the printed pattern was coated with glue and then sprinkled with lurex glitter. Like its forebears, the gown's skirt has swathes and drapes akin to elaborate curtain arrangements. Versace continued the tradition of designers such as Charles Frederick Worth and Charles James, but brought his creation firmly up-to-date with a pair of sturdy, workman-like 'braces'. The asymmetrically draped skirt parts to reveal glimpses of a pleated underskirt.

4

Spring/Summer 1993
Man's evening outfit, tail coat, waistcoat and jeans. Fine black wool gaberdine crêpe, black heavyweight cotton, black leather with gilt trimmings.

In iconoclastic mood, Versace mingled formal and informal components in an outfit for an aspiring rebel. A superbly tailored tail coat had its collar tipped with gilt in cowboy mode. Shirt and neckwear were completely eliminated, being replaced by an audacious collarless leather waistcoat, its zip-fastening front flanked by rows of corset-like lacing. A pair of sturdy jeans with pockets and flies flagrantly outlined in yellow top stitching were Versace's *coup de grace*.

5

Autumn/Winter 1986–87
Evening ensemble, top and skirt.
Black georgette embroidered with
silk and sequins, silk velvet with
heavy silk faille.

A body-hugging top with high
round neck and long sleeves is
embroidered all over with a
directional geometric pattern.
Sequinned and embroidered
rectangles radiate from the neck
and become larger towards the
waist. Resembling the silhouette of
a spinning top, the tapered skirt
consists of overlapping silk and
velvet bands – black on black.
In this ultra-sophisticated,
sensuously tactile composition,
sequins glitter against semi-glossy
embroidery, and matt silk vies
with the sheen of velvet pile.
(See Craft 39, p. 150)

6

Autumn/Winter 1986–87
Evening gown. Black silk with
openwork embroidery with
diamantés and bugle beads.

A full-length gown with a split
personality – the front has a
simple elegance with a floral
diamanté corsage, while the back
has seductive appeal. A glittering
openwork trellis forms the entire
top back panel, revealing
provocative glimpses of the naked
body. Hard, glinting and
geometric, the silver and black
openwork casts intriguing
shadows on the sensuous curves
beneath. To aid movement the
back skirt is inset with a widely-
flared kick panel. Versace kept
the black dress, little and
otherwise, in his repertoire,
and regularly experimented
with sexy backless garments.
(See Craft 40, p. 150)

7

Autumn/Winter 1990–91
Evening gown. Black acetate
(60%) and viscose (40%) jersey.

With characteristic bravura
Versace made this two-in-one
gala evening gown that was
guaranteed to raise all eyebrows.
From the front it appears to be
the ultimate in the 'covered-up'
look, comprised of an
asymmetrical, high neckline,
long sleeves (with small velvet
buttons) and ankle-length skirt.
In complete contrast, the back
has a brazen, convention-flouting
persona. Its horseshoe neckline
plunges to the bottom of the
spine where it meets the slit skirt,
revealing almost three-quarters
of the well nigh naked body.

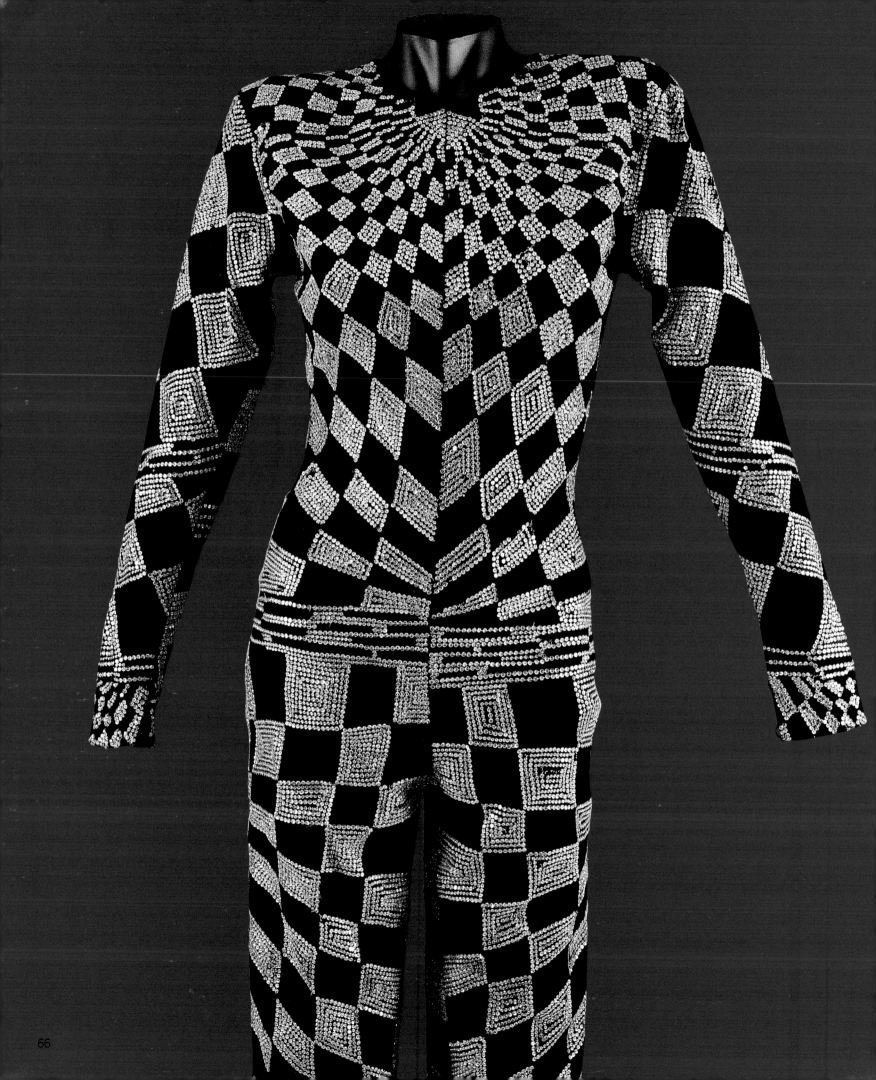

8

Autumn/Winter 1986–87
Catsuit. Hand-embroidered
(satin stitch and pulled thread)
and sequins on organza.

In this companion to the
embroidered top and layered
skirt (see p. 64), Versace created
a dazzling optical effect with black
and white geometrical squares
which have a logic of their own.
The squares radiating from the
neckline are carefully graduated
and angled to echo the contours
of a perfect body. The most
improbable of garments, the
catsuit becomes a decorative
second skin, requiring many
hours of painstaking embroidery
to achieve its effect.
(See Craft 39, p. 150)

9

Autumn/Winter 1996–97
Evening gown. Black, blue and
orange rayon jersey.

Versace used fabric with stretch to
hug the body's contours, and he
emphasized the garment's fluid
lines with inset serpentine panels.
The long, one-shouldered dress
with an orange-edged neckline
becomes a dynamic statement
(when viewed from the back) with
the simple addition of a sinuous
blue stripe that curves sugges-
tively over the derrière.

10

Spring/Summer 1989
Man's three-piece outfit, jacket,
trousers and waistcoat. Printed
shantung, black cotton, printed
linen.

In 1989 Versace discovered that
the technique of printing to shape
in one colour achieved the strong
results he required for that
season. Emulating designs found
on Balkan textiles and Celtic
artefacts, the bold prints were
equally successful as women's
gowns or men's waistcoats. A
printed narrow shawl collar makes
an otherwise conventional linen
jacket noteworthy, while the
crossover waistcoat has a
remarkably strong foliate pattern
that could never be overlooked.
(See Craft, Printing to Shape)

11

Spring/Summer 1992
Evening dress. Organza
overlaid with gold braid and
coloured stones, gold and
black fringing, beaded gold lace.

Ever intrigued with the
possibilities of theatrical and ballet
costume, Versace frequently
borrowed the form of the tutu for
his women's collections. In this
'vamp meets *jeune fille*', strictly
non-performance confection, he
teamed a plunging halter neck
and fitted bodice with bouffant
mini skirt. This extraordinarily
lavish design has a cornucopia of
textures in a predominantly gold
with black palette – even the
stiffened net petticoat is gold and
black with embroidered 'lace' at
the hem. (See Craft 49, p. 156)

12

Spring/Summer 1992
Evening ensemble, jacket and trousers. Black and white camouflage print with silk and gold thread with applied beaded motifs, printed and studded gold stretch silk lamé.

A simple jacket structure permitted Versace to concentrate entirely on three-dimensional surface embellishment. Recalling Schiaparelli's extraordinarily inventive approach to textural decoration (she also favoured gold for eveningwear), Versace created bristling horizontal layers of fringing beneath looped tiers of coarse gold net. The centre front fastening is concealed beneath a facing with a row of S-shaped motifs glittering with coloured stones, foil devices and beads; the curlicue motifs are repeated at the side front and on the sleeves.

13

Autumn/Winter 1990–91
Man's waistcoat and jeans. Printed silk crêpe embroidered with beads, studs and metallic threads.

With characteristic enterprise Versace took the technique of embroidery on a printed fabric to the extreme. His cherished 'Wild Baroque' print on fragile silk was embellished not with fine silks but with a variety of substantial metal threads normally used to decorate sturdy ceremonial uniforms. The ornate pattern of foliate coils, chrysanthemums and crowns is given a further dimension by the texture and glitter, transforming the waistcoat into an opulent special occasion garment.

14

Spring/Summer 1989
Evening ensemble, dress, waistcoat and bolero. Bright red pleated silk, hand-embroidery on chiffon (cut away) in red silk, sequins and bugle beads, hand-embroidery on tulle and chiffon in red silk diamantés and black and red beads and sequins.

From the first haute couture collection, a high-waisted, minuscule dress has a satin skirt with sun ray pleats which draw the eyes to the ensemble's main focus: the richly textured, highly decorated waistcoat and bolero. In red to match the dress, the waistcoat has a curvilinear, all-red foliate design which provides an ideal foil for the bolero's elaborate red and black floral paisley pattern. Edged with silvery beads, the long-sleeved bolero refers to bull fighters' magnificently embroidered suits and Balkan embroideries.

15

Autumn/Winter 1990–91
Trousers. Stretch tulle embroidered with polychromatic beads and sequins.

Inspired by a harlequin's costume brimming with verve and colour, a diamond trellis is beaded over the surface of a pair of slender trousers. In a clever interplay of black and white within coloured borders, most of the diamonds have central white dots and others enclose coloured motifs. Bright and dynamic, the trousers were set off on the catwalk by a simple black T-shirt and worn with 'resort' accessories: headscarf, big sunglasses and low shoes.

16

Autumn/Winter 1990–91
Hooded evening anorak. Black and red satin embroidered with beads and sequins.

Versace had shown prêt à porter anoraks in different colours and developed the idea for his haute couture collection. In glistening ebony satin, the back and long sleeves are heavily encrusted with semi-naturalistic floral swirls in vividly coloured beads, paillettes and glass stones. The beaded hood has a cosy, bright red quilted satin lining. With a circus-like finishing flourish, Versace gave the 'anorak' one green cuff and one red cuff.

17

Spring/Summer 1992
Evening ensemble, tail coat,
trousers and waistcoat similar to
the ensemble worn by Sting at his
marriage to Trudie Styler.
Black wool gaberdine crêpe,
beaded and braided black and
white printed satin.

A sharply tailored evening suit
proposed a variant on the
traditional tail coat, with its wide,
metal-tipped satin lapels, single-
link fastening and deeply curved
cutaway that set the blunt-ended
tails well behind the hips. A
beaded, chequered, high-
necked waistcoat provides a
dynamic accent to its suave
elegance. Even when in formal
mode, Versace could not resist
glamourizing his men.

18

Autumn/Winter 1995–96
Jacket worn by Elton John.
Black and white printed wool
crêpe embroidered with black and
silver sequins, black stones and
diamantés edged with black
paillettes and diamantés.

Throughout the 1970s and
1980s Elton John was renowned
for outrageously flamboyant stage
costumes (from a Day Glo
jumpsuit to a Donald Duck outfit).
By the 1990s he no longer
required the disguise of fantastic
costumes and found that
streamlined performance clothes
designed for him by Versace
suited his new, restrained mood.
Particularly effective was a refined
formula of a long-line, single-
breasted, four-buttoned jacket
with tapered trousers. Versace
made sure that the garments
retained extrovert characteristics
in their colour and pattern –
in addition to this glittering back
and white jacket, he made suits
in red and white check,
leopardskin print and bright pea
green PVC for Elton John.

19

Spring/Summer 1983
Evening dress. Silver-tone Oroton printed with blue flowers.

An early metal mesh dress shows how Versace mastered the new medium. He immediately treated it like the finest of pliant silks to achieve a body-conscious dress with a softly draped low décolletage supported by blue cotton straps and a skirt with flounces that cascade below the hemline. So determined was Versace to make this yardage versatile that he had drifting star-shaped flowers printed on the metal via a complicated resist process.

20

Autumn/Winter 1987–88
Evening gown. Black lacquered Oroton studded with diamantés, embroidered lace.

Ever fascinated with metallic mesh, Versace combined it with black lace in a sexy slip of a dress, which transformed a lingerie concept into ethereal eveningwear. This delicate semi-transparent slip top is reminiscent of exquisite 1930s underwear. Glistening metallic mesh is seductively draped about the hips over a lace skirt with a train, which gives the dress authority.

21

Autumn/Winter 1989–90
Evening gown. Black lacquered Oroton with diamantés.

A simply structured metal mesh gown has its considerable weight taken by one slender shoulder strap. Like drops of rain, lines of diamantés radiate from the neck down to the hem; they delineate the body's curves and enhance the glistening nature of the metal mesh.

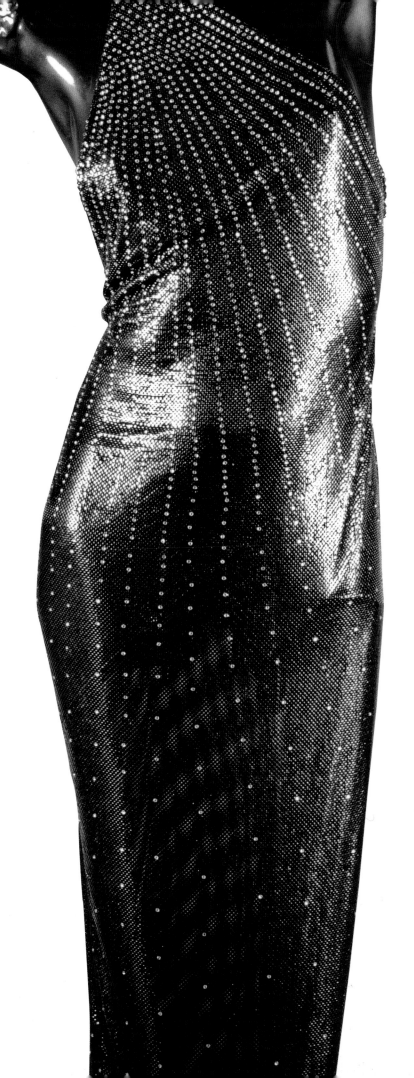

22

Spring/Summer 1994
Evening gown. Silver-tone Oroton.

Having worked with metal mesh for over a decade, Versace could make it do his bidding. This dress for a siren has a draped bodice (particularly successful in Oroton) and clings to the torso before falling in silvery flutes to an asymmetrical hem – long at the back and short at the front. The bodice is held aloft with a pair of 'braces' – an amusing and practical, punk-inspired ruse that recurred in Versace's 1990s collections.

23

Autumn/Winter 1997–98
Cocktail dress. Oroton, synthetic net and stones.

Always exploring the possibilities of metal mesh, Versace composed this slip of a dress with a plunging back U-neckline for his last collection. He continued to pursue the notion of underwear as outerwear in a draped chemise in which the solid mesh (embellished with black stones) of the central panel gives way to a see-through, lingerie-like foliate net side panel patterned with black stones. The strict grid of the metal mesh is relieved by the softly draped lines and embroidery. So revealing is this dress that underwear was restricted to a flesh-coloured g-string. Substantial snake-like padded shoulder straps support the exceedingly heavy garment.

24

Spring/Summer 1994
Evening dress. Crinkled silk satin and synthetic lace with gilt safety pins.

Versace played with the notion of intimate lingerie transformed into eveningwear in a number of collections. In this case he pushed things even further by treating the satin so that it appeared permanently crumpled, as if the wearer had been caught 'deshabillé'. The dress has an asymmetrical lace bodice and very full skirt of the finest satin lined with silk chiffon, and is slashed at the side. Versace used gilt pins to adorn the bodice, as if it were hastily fastened, enabling the dress to make the transition from illicit to public clothing.

25

Atelier Spring/Summer 1995
Evening gown worn by Madonna at The Brit Awards, 20 February 1995. Pleated silver grey satin with beaded sheer inserts.

Pleated, pearl-like satin flows without interruption from a fitted bodice. Painstakingly engineered knife-edged pleats cling to the torso and open gradually as they descend beyond the hips. Flared diaphanous inserts, embroidered with a graduated design of beads and iridescent paillettes, permit tempting glimpses of the legs beneath. A silvery composition in delicate fabrics, this gown alludes to the most luxurious of 1930s lingerie and eveningwear.

26

Spring/Summer 1997
Evening gown worn by Courtney Love. Ivory satin and chiffon.

Inspired by 1930s bias-cut gowns, particularly the work of Madeleine Vionnet, Versace created a dress that is almost angelic but at the same time dangerously provocative as it clings to every contour. The soft folds of the bodice front are caught in position by hidden stitches, while the shape of the plunging back neck is retained by light boning. Versace enhanced its fragility and simplicity with asymmetrical panels that float down the back.

27

Spring/Summer 1994
Prêt à porter. Man's evening
ensemble, jacket, shirt
and trousers. White wool
and safety pins.

Though far removed from its
street-style inspiration, this
exquisitely tailored jacket was
ideal for the urbane man aiming
for a classic look with a twist.
Three gilt Medusa-head buttons
fasten the single-breasted
front. One sleeve is slashed
from shoulder to wrist, while
the other has a slashed shoulder
seam. Both rents are secured
by bejewelled kilt pins, their
function to amuse and
disconcert rather than threaten.

Art

1

Autumn/Winter 1984–85
Evening gown. Black lacquered and copper Oroton with diamantés and amber stones.

Versace was preoccupied with the symbiotic relationship between the various arts and he regularly made garments with flat planes that could be treated as canvases. With verve he borrowed from the artists (both abstract and figurative) he most admired. Here, Klimt-like gold leaves drift across a metal mesh gown with a simple Kimono cut, draped softly at one side into a gilt bow. (See Craft 33, p. 147)

2

Spring/Summer 1997
Evening gown. Black and white hand-painted and appliquéd silk chiffon and georgette.

A slender, pillar-like strapless gown is composed of gossamer layers of a full-length white georgette (shot with metal threads) underdress and shorter black chiffon overdress. Curving around the body, a linear abstract pattern of tendrils and buds (glued satin appliqué) in black with occasional red highlights pays obeisance to the fragile mobiles of Alexander Calder.

3

Autumn/Winter 1989
Evening dress. Black synthetic net embroidered with multicoloured beads, diamantés and glass stones.

A simply constructed strapless gown with a bell-shaped skirt provided the perfect surface for this embroidered *tour de force*. Taking a lead from the costumes for *Java For Ever*, cosmological images, circus acrobats and horses mingle with geometric forms which celebrate the vibrantly coloured geometric work of abstract artists including Sonia and Robert Delaunay. Almost concealed in this abundance, the word ROCK is emblazoned across the skirt front.

4

Spring/Summer 1991
Catsuit. Silk and synthetic tulle with all-over multicoloured beadwork.

Versace created a catsuit with a difference by covering every inch of a second-skin garment with beads in an ebullient design depicting front covers of *Vogue* magazine. Beaded mannequins have their lips embroidered in bright red, eye-catching silk. Not for the shy and retiring, the bodysuit proclaimed the significance of this leading magazine, was great fun, and gave supermodels an opportunity to display their lithe physiques.

5

Spring/Summer 1991
Evening gown. Multicoloured printed silk.

In this slim halter neck gown, Versace paid homage to the central importance of *Vogue* as a magazine that recorded fashion and originated style. *Vogue* covers past and present were scattered over pliant silk that closely followed the body's curves. An uncomplicated cut (with thigh-high side slit and low V-back) gives prominence to the brightly coloured graphic print, though Versace could not resist embellishing the steeply cut-away arm holes with lavish beadwork.

6

September 1996
Evening gown and briefs.
Yellow synthetic devoré jersey.

Devoted to the theme 'Time and Fashion', the first Biennale di Firenze embraced seven wide-ranging exhibitions, including the show 'Art/Fashion' that occupied Fort Belvedere. As part of this investigation of the dialogue between art, architecture and fashion, a collaboration was established between the pop artist Lichtenstein and Versace (who collected Lichtenstein's work for his New York home). In this exuberant gown, Versace translated one of Lichtenstein's most famous paintings, 'Whaam!', of 1963, into a wearable form. It was displayed alongside a Lichtenstein sculpture.

7

Spring/Summer 1991
Evening dress. Multicoloured
printed silk twill with beadwork.

Versace's vividly coloured design
'L'artista' acknowledged his
passion for modern art and the
theatre. The vibrant abstract
pattern makes reference to
various modern art movements,
features the inscriptions 'pittora',
'artista' and 'arte', and encloses a
central harlequin figure. Initially
used for head squares, the print
was ideal for this vivacious little
dress in the tight bodice/short
bouffant skirt format that Versace
was so fond of. The strapless
bodice was stiffened by top
stitching, and further brio was
added through sparkling bead
embroidery around the midriff.
(See Craft 23, p. 140)

8

Spring/Summer 1991
Evening gown. Printed silk crêpe
with appliqué and beadwork.

This unapologetically extrovert
gown abounds with messages –
above all Versace's admiration
for the work of Andy Warhol, and
particularly his celebrity portraits.
Appropriately, Marilyn Monroe,
Hollywood's most prominent sex
symbol, and screen idol James
Dean adorn a body-revealing,
tightly fitted gown. To reinforce
the voluptuous mood, Versace
designed a bodice with beaded
straps and bustier top featuring
richly beaded and appliquéd
motifs that coil and meander
around the breasts.
(See Craft 8, p. 131)

9

Spring/Summer 1997
Day dress. Printed silk and
synthetic devoré.

A pert, scoop-necked, clinging
T-shirt dress is made remarkable
by a repeating pattern, in a
textured devoré technique, of
luscious red hearts alternating
with floral hearts in the style of
the pop artist Jim Dine.

History

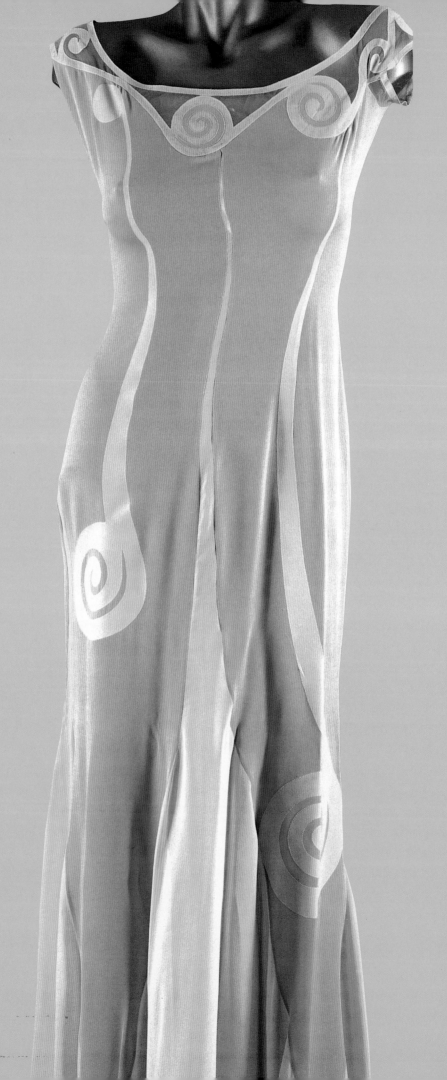

1

Spring/Summer 1997
Evening gown. Acid yellow
and lilac silk chiffon.

An enchanting dress for sultry
nights has long lilac panels
with Mycenaean-like applied
decoration. Fullness in the lower
skirt is achieved by flared
insets of yellow chiffon. A watery
mood is evoked by wave-like
serpentine scrolls and
transparent inset panels of
stiffened tulle at the neckline.

2

Spring/Summer 1997
Evening gown. Mustard and yellow
ochre silk chiffon with gold print.

An unpretentious, body-
skimming slip of a dress in
tranquil colours has its willowy
nature emphasized by inset
tapering stripes. Printed gold
meanders and stripes decorate
neck and waist, while inlaid semi-
transparent tulle panels give the
bodice a slightly risqué touch.
Richard Martin drew attention
to its Art Deco palette and
mentioned the influence of
Mycenaean art in the
Metropolitan Museum of Art's
catalogue of the exhibition
'Gianni Versace', December
1997–March 1998.

3

Autumn/Winter 1997–98
Evening gown and body. Yellow
viscose jersey, black leather
and Lycra.

In a striking double-identity
columnar gown, Versace made
reference to the high-waisted
Directoire style popular
between 1908 and 1910, and to
the asymmetrical draping
favoured in the 1930s. While the
jersey overdress carries subtle
hints of the work of Paul Poiret
and Madame Grès, the strapless
leather body is undeniably
Versace. Maximum impact is
achieved by setting supple,
loose-fitting, acid yellow jersey
against tight black leather.

4

Autumn/Winter 1997–98
Evening gown. Rose pink
silk cady.

A sleeveless gown clings
seductively to the body's
contours. Supple jersey forms a
draped U-shaped neckline, below
which the dress is softly gathered
across the torso into a curved
seam along the right side to thigh
level and is then open to the hem
in a leg-revealing slit. Versace
drew upon draped and gently
pleated eveningwear of the 1930s
and 1940s, in particular the work
of Madame Grès. From Versace's
last collection, the gown was
modelled by Naomi Campbell
at Donna Sotto Le Stelle –
the yearly event in Rome at which
major fashion designers show
their most important pieces.

5

Spring/Summer 1995
Evening gown. Pale blue
nylon jersey.

While creating this exercise in the
art of pleating, Versace had in
mind the draped garments of
ancient Greece and Rome and, in
particular, various provocative
(often fanciful) reinterpretations of
classical costume in post-war
movies. Double straps buckled
back and front support the low-
necked bustier top. Versace
manipulated soft pleats three
ways in this brief and seductive
garment, with its plunging
décolletage and handkerchief-
pointed skirt that is saucily thigh-
high on one side but demurely
floor length on the other.

6

Atelier Spring/Summer 1995
Evening dress. Silk georgette
lamé, synthetic net, chiffon.

The finely pleated bodice of this
evening gown evokes the calm,
classically inspired work of
Madame Grès. In contrast the
layered skirts are animated by the
restless, curling movement of the
rolled edges of the fabric. Versace
treats the expensive silk so that it
resembles synthetic fabric, while
the normally concealed petticoat
becomes a visible part of the
composition. Substantial buckled
straps abruptly update the dress.

7

Spring/Summer 1992
Ensemble, bustier, jacket, jeans
and belt. Embroidered, appliquéd,
braided and beaded pale blue silk
faille moiré, indigo denim.

Versace frequently emphasized
the sensuality of luxurious garments
by teaming them with utilitarian
relatives. Thus he put a pair of denim
jeans with a precious, baby blue,
tailored, braid-edged silk moiré
jacket encrusted with lavish
curlicues in gold thread, appliqué,
sequins and beads. A huge floral
roundel enclosing a trio of
embroidered ballerinas adorns the
jacket's back, while a matching blue
crêpe and tulle bustier is lavishly
decorated with gold and blue beads.

8

Spring/Summer 1992
Evening ensemble, shirt and
skirt. Indigo denim, printed gold,
black and white silk faille and
gold and lurex lace.

Versace teamed a sturdy, two-
pocket workwear denim shirt (top
stitched in gold) with a delicate, full-
length, layered silk and lace skirt.
The latter, in a print based upon an
18th-century original, is divided into
panels held together with black
bows over the flowery lace. The
polymath Versace delighted in such
incongruous blends, regularly
issuing the question 'Why not?'.

9

Spring/Summer 1992
Evening ensemble, dress,
petticoats and jacket. Printed Gazar,
gold lace (silk, nylon and polyester),
indigo denim.

A perky short dress has a fitted
bodice with low neckline and full
skirt, box-pleated into the nipped-in
waist. A youthful design (originally for
a scarf), it is carefully composed to
accommodate the figurative pattern
of dancers within roundels adapted
from historical studies – including a
quartet of 19th-century ballerinas.
Teamed with a customized cropped
denim jacket with gold top stitching
and Medusa-head gilt buttons, it
attains a post-modern look.

10.

Autumn/Winter 1997-98
Wedding dress. Silver and Oroton

11.

Autumn/Winter 1997-98
Cocktail dress. Black leather
embroidered with amber beads.

Simple short-sleeved minikle
unlivened by an asymmetrical
neckline delineated by a chunky
Roman braiding and, over the right
hip, a large golden Greek
cross. Richard Martin (Gianni
Versace, 1997) explained that
Versace was inspired by the
Metropolitan Museum of Art's
exhibition "The Glory of
Byzantium" to revisit themes he
had pursued in the early 1990s.
Without sacrilegious intent, the
designer was interested in the
impact of the cross when used as
a purely decorative motif in a
secular context.

12

Autumn/Winter 1991–92
Evening ensemble, jacket, top
and skirt. Embroidered black
nappa leather, astrakan, pleated
chiffon and satin.

In the post-war period fashion
designers gleaned inspiration
from a universal visual spectrum,
including, most significantly, the
arts of the past. Little has escaped
their laser-like scan and little is
sacrosanct. Versace spotted the
rich potential of fusing ecclesiastical images and fashion. On a
bejewelled halter neck top he
redefined and paid homage to the
richness of religious icons and
mosaics in enormous, brightly
coloured glass stones and beads.
The jacket with an astrakan collar
has its shoulders, back and arms
adorned with motifs in the form of
crosses. (See Craft 45, p. 154)

13

Autumn/Winter 1991–92
Evening ensemble, bolero, shirt,
jeans, belt. Beaded and
embroidered tulle, printed silk,
indigo denim.

In an explosion of colour and texture
Versace ignored the notions of
symmetry and scale, making
religious images of Madonna and
Child and the Crucifix into a joyful
celebration of ecclesiastical art and
decoration for secular consumption.
He crammed many types of beads,
sequins, large stones, foil motifs and
paillettes together, composed silk-
embroidered fronds and employed
as much pattern as possible to
create a jewel of a garment. Even the
lining is a brightly patterned silk twill
printed with icons. It was originally
worn over a multicoloured silk shirt
with a pair of tight indigo jeans
fastened with a deep, bejewelled
belt. (See Craft 19, p. 138)

14

1993
Bridal coat designed for Francesca Von Thyssen. Ivory cashmere embroidered with beads, pearls, diamantés and gold threads and braid.

Most appropriately for the marriage of an aristocrat to a son of the House of Hapsburg, Versace based the bride's romantic ivory and gold ensemble on the dashing uniform of an officer of the Austrian Empire. Based on a military redingote, the lavishly trained, deluxe coat was given resplendent embroidered satin collar, cuffs and pockets. Though the fastening is single breasted, Versace created a double-breasted look (at back and front) with decorative corset-like, top-stitched satin lacing giving the garment a feminine flourish.

15

Spring/Summer 1988
Evening gown. Printed and machine-quilted yellow silk.

An extraordinary gown has a delicate fitted bodice and a long, pod-like skirt that swells out over the hips then tapers to the hem. It was conceived as a tribute to the maestro Paul Poiret and the inventive garments he designed around 1910–12 under the influence of Orientalism. Poiret would have approved of the yellow/purple colour combination as well as the printed and quilted carnations. Versace borrowed volume, shape and colours from Poiret and translated them into a gown for the late 1980s. Concept was paramount – the bodice was cool but though it is lightweight, the quilted skirt would have been rather warm on hot summer nights.

16

Autumn/Winter 1988–89
Evening gown. Quilted black velveteen, embroidered silk voile.

Intrigued by Paul Poiret's work as well as Oskar Schlemmer's analyses of clothing and volume which culminated in *The Triadic Ballet* of 1922, Versace gave this gown an immense ovoid skirt. He observed the convention of a fitted bodice with deep décolletage (with boned, rolled satin edge), but the ballooned skirt defied the norm. Sumptuous velvet quilted with a diamond trellis as well as a floral design adds other tactile dimensions to this phenomenal garment. Peeping out below the hem are embroidered leggings, an acknowledgement of Poiret's attempts to promote trousers for women.

17

Spring/Summer 1988
Evening ensemble, top, skirt and belt. Mauve and lilac beaded and embroidered synthetic tulle, printed silk faille.

A tightly fitted, semi-transparent sleeveless top with a sparkling embroidered floral pattern is anchored by a deep grosgrain belt above a leg-revealing, exuberant, asymmetrical skirt of layered bouffant panels. Judicious padding and folded layers help to shape the faille skirt and give it volume. Its structure is reminiscent of certain late 18th- and 19th-century skirts, and its romantic aura is enhanced by a pattern of naturalistic full-blown roses in shades of mauve and lilac.

18

Spring/Summer 1982
Evening dress. Beaded and printed multicoloured silk chiffon.

An ethereal dress for summer nights consists of a delicate double layer of chiffon wrapped sarong-like to form a tube which is secured at the centre front. The asymmetrical hem is elegantly long at the back and short at the front. The cylindrical shape evokes the 1920s and, in keeping with this mood, the top has a deep printed and lightly beaded border of a geometric pattern derived from Art Deco motifs.

19

Autumn/Winter 1990–91
Evening ensemble, bodice and skirt. Black net embroidered with multicoloured silks, sequins and diamantés, satin, duchesse satin and faille printed with various black and white geometric patterns.

Versace excelled at extrovert gestures in which he compelled apparently discordant parts to work together. Thus a startlingly bright, polychromatic, pretty floral body partners a skirt of ruthlessly precise black and white checks. Within a shape influenced by 1950s eveningwear, the strapless top with a Rococo spirit meets a skirt in the black and white of 1960s Op Art. The embroidery is lavishly three-dimensional, with layered petals, satin stitch, sequins and stones. A *tour de force* in its volume and complexity, the skirt (with stiff interlinings) is composed of five different black and white geometric designs arranged in bouffant layers, volants and flounces.

Theatre

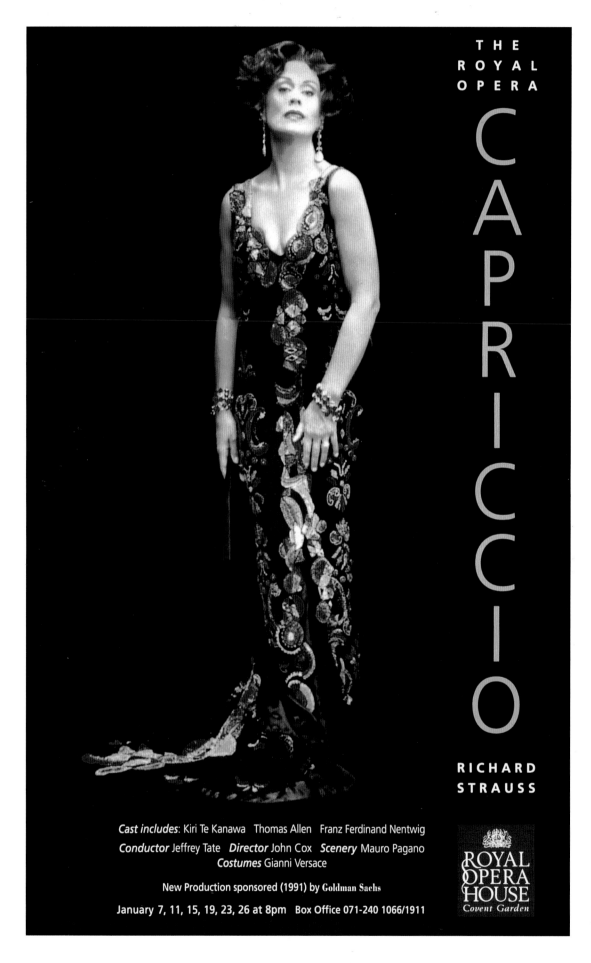

THE ROYAL OPERA

CAPRICCIO

RICHARD STRAUSS

Cast includes: Kiri Te Kanawa Thomas Allen Franz Ferdinand Nentwig
Conductor Jeffrey Tate *Director* John Cox *Scenery* Mauro Pagano
Costumes Gianni Versace

New Production sponsored (1991) by Goldman Sachs

January 7, 11, 15, 19, 23, 26 at 8pm Box Office 071-240 1066/1911

ROYAL OPERA HOUSE
Covent Garden

1

1989
Theatre costume worn by Dame Kiri Te Kanawa. Black satin embroidered with bugle beads, beads and silk. *Capriccio*.

A gown for a diva, this full-length, heavily embroidered masterpiece was an ideal vehicle for Versace, with his love of drama and applied decoration. Understanding the mechanics of the stage, he made a gown with an imposing train that was impressive from both front and back. Vertical lines of vividly hued, embroidered, semi-naturalistic motifs on a black ground (reminiscent of 1920s Chinese export embroidery) give the wearer height and power.

2

1984
Man's dance costume. Bright red silk, wool and satin. *Dionysus*.

Versace returned to a style he had first investigated in 1982 for vividly coloured cotton Bermuda shorts. The cut was based on the traditional attire of Balinese dancers and, in brilliant red, these trousers – for the dancer in the role of Dionysus – became a powerful statement on stage at La Scala, Milan. The pointed sides were achieved by pleating flat panels of fabric into the waist. For dramatic purposes Versace made the waistband extra deep, above which the dancer's torso was left naked.

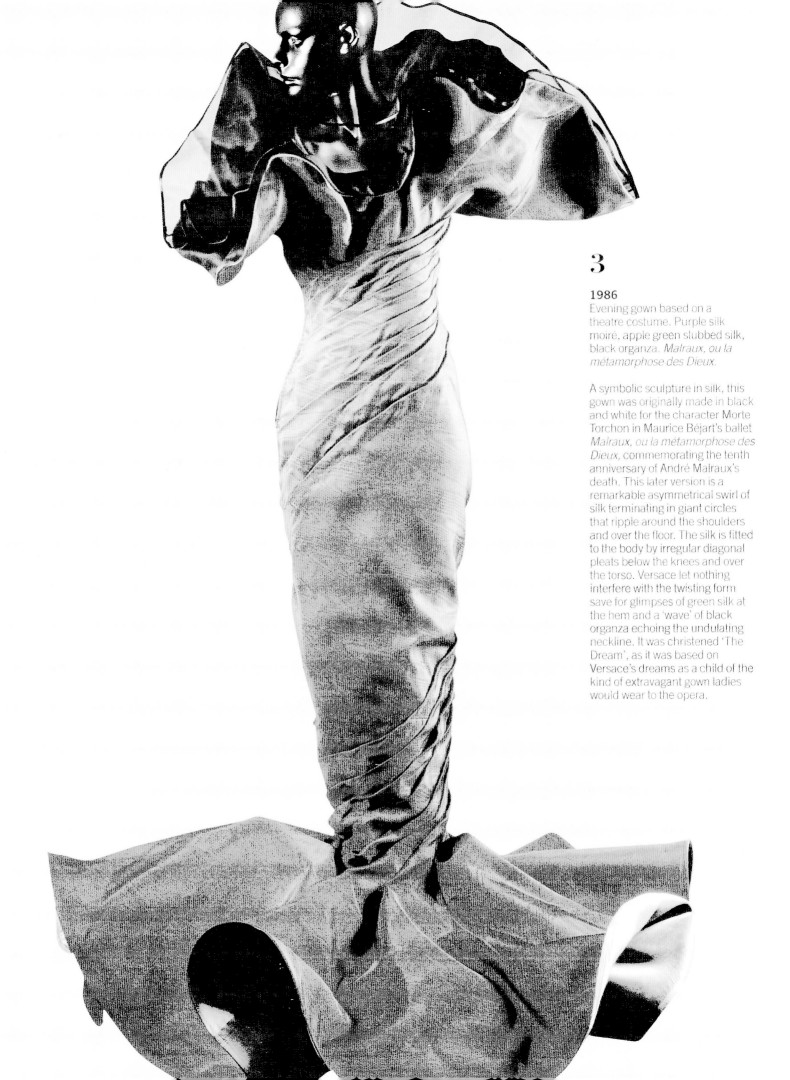

3

1986
Evening gown based on a theatre costume. Purple silk moiré, apple green slubbed silk, black organza. *Malraux, ou la métamorphose des Dieux*.

A symbolic sculpture in silk, this gown was originally made in black and white for the character Morte Torchon in Maurice Béjart's ballet *Malraux, ou la métamorphose des Dieux*, commemorating the tenth anniversary of André Malraux's death. This later version is a remarkable asymmetrical swirl of silk terminating in giant circles that ripple around the shoulders and over the floor. The silk is fitted to the body by irregular diagonal pleats below the knees and over the torso. Versace let nothing interfere with the twisting form save for glimpses of green silk at the hem and a 'wave' of black organza echoing the undulating neckline. It was christened 'The Dream', as it was based on Versace's dreams as a child of the kind of extravagant gown ladies would wear to the opera.

4

1987
Dance costume. Woollen cloth with silk satin appliqués embroidered with silk thread and diamantés. Tights in Lycra embroidered with silk thread, pearls and diamanté. *Souvenir de Leningrad.*

This two-piece costume was worn by a dancer in the role of a prince in Maurice Béjart's ballet *Souvenir de Leningrad*, performed at the Palais de Beaulieu, Lausanne. The simple top has a stiffened peplum and long sleeves with pointed cuffs – the focus is upon bold foliate motifs and scrollwork, echoed in beaded and braided panels on the stretch acrylic heavyweight tights. Using a simple formula with a limited colour palette, Versace achieved a great effect.

5

1987
Dance costume.
Hand-painted and appliquéd silks. *Souvenir de Leningrad.*

This magnificent stage costume for *Souvenir de Leningrad* verges on caricature but is thrilling in its volume and layer upon layer of colour and pattern. Work for the theatre enabled Versace to run riot making costumes where excess was an absolute necessity. Russian dress inspired this ensemble, with its vast skirt, lacquer red bodice and towering head-dress. It has strength akin to Iosif Shpinel's costumes for Eisenstein's *Ivan the Terrible* epics.

6

1987
Dance costume.
Ecru linen with cutwork.
Souvenir de Leningrad.

For Maurice Béjart's dance
Souvenir de Leningrad,
performed at the Palais du
Beaulieu, Lausanne, Versace
took elements from Russian art,
architecture and dress and
created tutus in cream on cream
with touches of silver. In this
costume the audience was
permitted glimpses of
beribboned drawers that peep
below the bouffant skirt with a
sweetly scalloped hem.
Immaculately tucked and
ruffled, the all-cream bodice is
an exercise in refined texture.

7

1987
Dance costume. Ecru linen
embroidered to shape with
silk, diamantés and beads.
Souvenir de Leningrad.

Another monochromatic, dainty
tutu for *Souvenir de Leningrad*
in carefully embroidered linen is
reminiscent of delicate fashions
worn by young girls in the late
19th century. Although this
costume had to withstand the
rigours of the stage, Versace
used fine stitches to ornament
scalloped tiers of pure (easy to
crease) linen; he eschewed the
cruder decorative techniques
and sturdier fabrics normally
employed by theatrical
costumiers.

8

1987
Theatre costume.
Ivory and black silk and
organza. *Salome.*

Versace made the most of
striking black and ivory in this
ensemble for Herodias in Richard
Strauss's *Salome*, performed at
La Scala, Milan. The long,
pillar-like gown in ivory silk is
bisected by a black silk line down
the centre front. Enjoying the
freedom of stage costume and
echoing the work of Capucci,
Versace placed enormous
rectangular shoulder extensions
in pleated black Lycra over the
gown. A full-length, cascading
organza train completed the
dramatic composition.

9

1987
Theatre costume.
Black velveteen and black
silk taffeta. *Salome.*

Everything could be hugely
exaggerated for the theatre, and
Versace was at liberty to ruche
glossy black taffeta in giant irregular
formations to achieve this
somewhat forbidding costume for
Salome at La Scala. Though it has
roots in the 1930s, the costume was
also inspired by 1950s designs by
Balenciaga and Dior. The ruched
satin shoulders and trained,
diagonally-set skirt make the torso
look extremely slender. Though
Versace had fun with the taffeta, he
otherwise showed great restraint
and employed just one decorative
touch at the waist: a silver motif
with delicate teardrop pearls.

10

1978

Theatre costume. Black and white organza and silk. *Salome*.

It was only to be expected that Versace's Alice in Wonderland would wear chic white with black rather than the traditional blue and white established by Tenniel's illustrations for *The Nursery Alice*, 1889. Versace rang the changes on the 'little girl dress' with fitted bodice and flounced skirt by introducing large, squared sleeves, a demure Peter Pan collar and saucy bow positioned over the posterior. Black edging and trimming on white give the pert dress dramatic appeal and a worldly rather than an innocent quality.

11

1988

Dance costume. Black silk chiffon embroidered with sequins, beads, diamantés and coloured stones, black silk fringing. *Java For Ever*.

Versace designed the costumes for the ballet *Java For Ever*, choreographed by Roland Petit, starring Petit's wife Zizi Jeanmaire, and performed at the Theatre Bouffes du Nord, Paris. This tightly-fitting, short black dress, with its asymmetrical deeply fringed hem, emphasized Zizi Jeanmaire's gamine beauty and taut dancer's body. The whole composition, with 'Java For Ever' emblazoned in brilliant colours on sparkling black and the swinging fringe, was seen to best advantage when in movement.

12

1988

Man's dance costume. Black synthetic crin embroidered with multicoloured sequins, glass stones and diamantés, white Lycra. *Java For Ever*.

For the modern ballet *Java For Ever*, Versace produced another variation on the diamond-shaped 'Oriental' pantaloons he had been experimenting with since 1982. Customary pleats at the waist were avoided in order to give free rein to the colourful, glittering pattern and the trousers were boned to keep their shape. Worn over white, high-waisted tights they accompanied the prima ballerina's costume, beaded with similar ebullient motifs gleaned from abstract art, cosmological images and the circus.

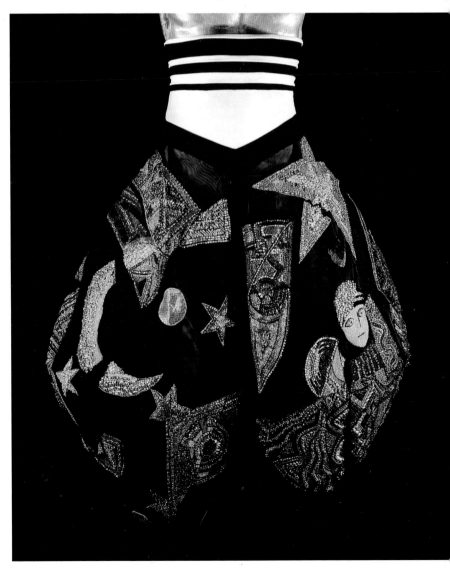

13

1989
Dance costume.
Cream and black silk and satin with satin velvet and net appliqué. *Elegie pour Elle.*

For a dancer representing a doll in the ballet *Elegie pour Elle* by Maurice Béjart, Versace made a youthful little dress with a striking geometric design carried out in a restricted palette of black, grey and cream. A *jeune fille* bodice has short puffed sleeves and the crinoline skirt, held aloft by layered petticoats, is gathered into a nipped-in waist and bells out to a deep border of abstract motifs.

14

1989
Theatre costume, jacket and skirt. Black quilted satin and white satin with black and white appliqué. *Capriccio.*

Worn by Clairon in Richard Strauss's opera *Capriccio* at the Opera House, San Francisco, this authoritative exercise in black and white had its roots in Versace's glamorous evening collections, but all the elements became larger than life. The designer assembled favourite ideas in the off-the-shoulder bodice decorated with whorls over the breasts and with a tantalizing plunging neckline. To this he added an immense skirt based on historical dress and ornamented with a striking curvilinear pattern given a third dimension with padded arabesques and couched lines of heavy cord.

15

1991
Theatre costume. Man's outfit, coat, waistcoat and breeches. Lime green embroidered silk faille, silk grosgrain in pinks, red, blues and green hand-painted and embroidered with metallic threads (waistcoat), quilted purple silk. *Capriccio.*

Ostentatious 18th-century men's attire was the springboard for this ebullient costume worn by one of the musicians in Richard Strauss's *Capriccio* at the Royal Opera House, Covent Garden. Using historical dress as his template, Versace exaggerated the components to achieve an ensemble that glories in vivid contrasting colours and pantomime-like features. Huge buttons, faux buttonholes and turnback cuffs adorn the lime green coat, while bright purple breeches are quilted in bold diagonals and the waistcoat's vast sun heads sparkle with metal threads. Like so much of his work for the theatre this was an ideal commission for Versace, who adored to give styles of the past new identities.

black buttons along its left side, while in counterpoint a detachable black sleeve (not shown) has a row of inoperative white buttons. Abstract art invaded the costume in a Miro-like appliqué pattern that sweeps across the flared skirt, and in a multicoloured cubist design painted on a flat, crescent-shaped accompanying head-dress.

16

1991
Theatre costume. Hand-painted, quilted and appliquéd polychromatic silks. *Capriccio*.

In a principal's costume for *Capriccio* at the Royal Opera House, London, micro techniques of quilting and top stitching were married to theatrical 'big brush' processes. Versace employed a huge, floor-sweeping skirt to give the character a lofty presence and to act as a canvas for an abstract 'painting'. Dividing the back skirt into a black and white side and a polychromatic side (with startling electric blue and vivid purple), he introduced texture and play of light and shade with diamond quilting and closely spaced parallel lines of top stitching.

17

1989
Theatre costume. Gown. Ecru satin with black and grey appliqué. *Dr Faustus*.

A spectacular costume relied on a powerful design in a restricted palette. Small details count even in theatrical costume – the fitted ivory bodice has a line of non-functional but graphically compelling

18

1987 (see page 102)
Dance costume. Tutu and top.
Aigrette and chicken feathers,
tulle, beads. *Souvenir de
Leningrad.*

In a costume for a princess,
Versace teamed a brightly
coloured, stiff tutu of blue and
red feathers and layered tulle
which would respond to the
dancer's slightest movement, with
an embroidered and brightly
beaded top in the form of a bird
with outstretched wings, to create
the most exotic of outfits.

19

1991
Dance costume. Tutu, skirt and
leotard. Silk satin, synthetic
organza, gold braiding and
feathers. Leotard in hand-painted
Lycra. *The Carnival for the Birds.*

Versace created this costume for
the 'Firebird' for a gala benefit
performance of *The Carnival for
the Birds*, performed at the Royal
Opera House, Covent Garden in
1991. The red bodice of the
brightly coloured tutu is
encrusted with gold bugle beads
and paillettes which form a
semi-military pattern of
horizontal bands. The top skirt
has appliqué whorls and flowers
edged with gold beads and
ornamented with large coloured
stones. The underskirt is hand-
painted with geometrical shapes
in primary colours outlined in
gold and is supported by a
stiffened red net and gold lace
petticoat. The tutu is worn over a
hand-painted leotard creating a
dynamic and vibrant ensemble.

Donatella Versace

1

Spring/Summer 2000
Evening gown. Blue and green printed silk chiffon with a jewelled clasp by Swarovski.

Donatella excels in the Versace tradition of dressing show-business celebrities in sensational gowns for special occasions. Jennifer Lopez made the headlines when she displayed this body-revealing creation at the Grammy Awards. It plunged down the centre front beyond her navel to a single gem cluster fastening and then fluttered open to the ground. In bright green and blue the 'jungle' print was seen to its best advantage against the star's glowing skin and sensual curves.

2

Autumn/Winter 2001–02
Evening gown. Lilac silk chiffon embroidered with iridescent sequins and diamantés.

In an ultra-feminine mood, Donatella Versace employed soft colours, fluid chiffon and sparkling embroidery to create a delicate evening gown. Narrow straps support the dress that is fitted to thigh level before godets of pleated, shimmering chiffon fan out to the hem, which is short at the front and sweeps to floor level at the back. A linear embroidered cobweb of gentle arcs curve across the torso in directional contrast to the fanned, vertical pleats of the lower skirt. Its precise knife pleating is softened by a delicate edging of floral motifs.

3

Spring/Summer 2002
Cocktail dress. Black leather.

Supple black napa leather is moulded tightly over the contours to form a demure from the front/audacious from the back, evening sheath with deeply cut-away arm holes. Donatella Versace gave the gleaming leather added appeal with decorative detailing: surface stitching emphasizes long, curved seams, punched lattice work comprises a see-through yoke and saucy fringing draws attention to the narrow hem (slit along the centre back to allow movement). The 'very Versace' cut-out top back panel scoops low enough to allow a provocative glimpse of the buttocks. Black leather thonging laces the cut-out panel's curved edges (shaped to highlight a narrow waist) and ties in a bow over the posterior.

The Craft of Gianni Versace

The Craft of Gianni Versace by Chiara Buss

Gianni Versace often used to say that: 'My earliest memory is of a black velvet dress. I must have been about nine years old.' It was not the dress's shape, nor its form, nor how it was designed to be worn, nor even its decorative details; it was the material and colour of the dress being fitted in his mother's atelier that stuck in the young boy's imagination.

As many fashion experts have remarked, right from the beginning of his career, Versace always paid a great deal of attention to the materials he used, an interest that developed from his in-depth cultural and technical knowledge of fabrics. To add to this expertise, he had an unbridled curiosity, which, as he himself admitted, was almost childlike: 'Sometimes I see aspects of my mother in Donatella and elements of my father in Santo, but I always see myself as the little boy.' This curiosity led him on a journey of spatial and temporal exploration, as much into the future as into the past, in his search for different cultural traditions to adopt and adapt. His thirst for appropriation was an act of love, which, like love itself, translated into a desire to modify the object of his passion, recreating it afresh.

It would only be telling half the story to say that Versace's choice of materials was inspired by the past, just as it would be oversimplifying things to state, as others have done, that Versace invented new materials. In fact, Versace reinvented what he and others knew and loved, metabolically transforming them into materials that were both new and totally his.

The process of reinventing materials is obviously reflected in the shapes and forms of Versace's clothes, but is particularly evident at two discrete stages in the development of a material and it follows several different procedures. The first stage is the act of direct intervention at the time the material is being made; the second is the moment when it is decided how the material will be used. The procedures are related to processes of replacement, overlapping, layering, blending and transposition of individual elements relating to technique, history and geography as well as to both the material and symbolic contexts of the fabric. They are also linked to concepts of sexual, social and historical role reversal and to contrasting combinations of techniques, materials and shapes.

The Making of the Material

When considering direct intervention in the production of the material itself, it is essential to clarify the extent to which a stylist can influence the actual making of the material. In the majority of cases, textile manufacturers present fashion designers with a vast range of textiles each season, and it is the designer who narrows down the selection, choosing the textures, patterns and colours best suited to transforming his idea into shapes and volumes. He often introduces only marginal variations so that the resulting material remains in-keeping with his own style. Very often these variations aim to neutralize an overly characterful fabric, as too flamboyant a fabric can detract from the designer's formal concept. But Versace intervened in the most fundamental aspects of the fabric itself, involving himself with the yarns and their blends, the weave, the pattern and the finish. He frequently asked for the fabrics to be put through unprecedented processes in order to achieve something that had never been done before. Rather than choose any of the samples shown to him, he let them serve as trials for the fabrics he wanted.

Versace first experimented with woven fabrics in his Autumn/Winter 1983–84 collection, for which he introduced the concept of replacement as a simplifying strategy. He asked for patterns to be produced in a twill weave with tweed yarns to achieve prominent coloured areas. This resulted in a striped effect rather than the usual speckled mix of colours; Versace had succeeded in inventing a pattern that was completely new to tweed. The following winter, he combined the ancient manual technique of padding with the nineteenth-century technique of double weave. This hailed a multitude of variations: binding either on the weft or on the warp that produced checks or diminishing degrees of vaulted ribs; shaded warps to create additional chromatic effects; and countless variations of the principles of blending and layering.

Pursuing the theme of layering, on this occasion linking the idea to layering several sheets of fabric on top of each other, for Autumn/Winter 1988–89 Versace padded a Prince of Wales woollen check and embroidered it with acanthus leaves. He succeeded in combining this severely geometric pattern with the most sinuous of Baroque motifs. The traditionally smooth surface of fine worsted with a Prince of Wales check was violated by the crude relief of the thick cotton embroidery. It constituted the perfect overlapping of decorative elements from different periods and contexts and brought together contradictory sartorial and textile traditions.

Precisely because it stands for a long textile tradition as well as male conservatism, the Prince of Wales check was a recurring target for Versace's experimentation with contrasting combinations. In 1994, Versace commissioned the pattern in a weave incorporating slits which reinforced the checked rhythm of the pattern, but interrupted its smooth surface. The following year, he subjected a classic Prince of Wales check to a polyurethane print finish, which coated the surface with irregular black and iridescent polka dots. In the Spring/Summer 1998 collection, Versace's sister Donatella paid homage to one of her brother's favourite themes. She cut weft threads and removed them by hand to create a distressed look that was stabilized by hand-embroidering with 'invisible' threads. The technique was applied to minimalist strapless evening dresses for which the traditional Prince of Wales check had never before been used.

Continuing his sacrilegious approach to traditional menswear fabrics, Versace subjected the ultra-classic pin-stripe to both a material and a formal transposition for his Spring/Summer 1986 collection. Instead of using the customary wool, he produced it in linen with a finish which gave it a crumpled effect, thus subverting the main feature of pin-stripe worsted wool – the perfect hang. This idea follows in the vein of Oscar Wilde's dictates about true elegance: the ruffled and slightly damaged appearance of the fabric results from the wearer's blatant disregard for the expense of the garment. This idea became a staple of Versace's highly referential repertoire with womenswear as well, right up until his final collections. On the subject of material transposition and technical substitution, one of Versace's most innovative developments was the use of printing to shape instead of the more familiar hand-embroidering of the finished garment. He replaced the embroidery that customarily delineates hem, neckline, cuffs, edges and pockets with a decoration printed in the piece. The smooth effect of a machine-printed pattern replaced three-dimensional embroidery executed by hand.

A silk fabric that featured in the Spring/Summer 1986 collection was perhaps the most important example of overlapping and blending. It recalls elephant's hide, the first of many references to animal skin that would appear in Versace's work right through to his last collections. In this instance, a woven silk was discharge printed and then heat-finished to obtain the rough texture and colour of animal skin, belying the smoothness of the silk. In the same collection, a black and white print suggested rhinoceros hide, and the hand-applied opaque gold areas were unmistakable references to splashes of mud. The latter is perhaps one of the most sophisticated examples of how Versace liked to create the effect of animal hide, without directly imitating it. It is his playful attitude towards transposing material and chromatic elements which distinguishes his entire iconographic repertoire. His interest in animal skin evolved and culminated in the 'Wild Baroque' motif of 1991, in which he combined spotted fur with golden volutes of Baroque acanthus leaves. In the following years, he went on to employ spotted fur as if it were the most natural backdrop to the numerous other decorative themes of his prints, such as the views of Miami and the shells series. In the final years, he exaggerated these combinations still further, taking them right out of their historical, social and geographical context.

He treated real animal skin as if it were fabric with the same determination with which he had transformed silk into animal skin. In Autumn/Winter 1982–83, he dyed it red and covered it with metal studs. The following season, he dyed and printed leather to look like crocodile skin, and then used it for slinky garments. By using one of the softest materials available – aniline-treated leather – he created long overcoats that evoke the movement of a coriaceous crocodile. Still intrigued by role reversal, in 1992 he padded leather as though it were fabric and then, in 1994, he treated it to a crumpling process as if it were linen.

For his Autumn/Winter 1983–84 collection he began to experiment with rubber. Using heat to imprint patterns of lozenges and bands, and synthetic jersey to line it, he transformed rubber into trousers, jackets, berets and gloves, creating fashionable clothes whose potential for keeping the wearer warm was unprecedented. Previously, rubber had only been used for performance sportswear and professional protective clothing, or for shoes, but with Versace, rubber became part of the everyday wardrobe; it was a prime example of his talent for transposing the use of a material.

Twelve years later, Versace used a material that was traditionally even further removed from the world of fashion: vinyl. For Autumn/Winter 1995–96, he limited himself to using it on the pockets and bib of a simple white crêpe woollen dress. However, the following summer saw an irreverent explosion of vinyl in the form of a long dress with an enormous train, and in the winter Versace used it as the transparent ground for his short tunics covered in Swarovski diamantés. Vinyl and diamantés was a typical out-of-context combination – the one a utilitarian 'fabric', the other glittering emblems of sumptuous fashion.

While Versace's use of rubber and plastic was more of a provocative experiment than a serious fashion proposal, metal mesh came to symbolize the apex of his creative ability in terms of materials. For Autumn/Winter 1982–83, inspired by medieval soldiers' coats of mail, he completed research which led to the invention of Oroton. Once again, he was applying the principles of role reversal and historical transposition. A metal mesh that was similar to its historical prototype was used for making a man's 'corselet' to be worn under a leather jacket. The same mesh was repeated on the jacket's shoulders and sleeves and was intended to give the wearer the air of a rugged, aggressive warrior. Versace went on to discover other means of expressing male aggression in his later collections, but for womenswear he relentlessly pursued the idea of metal mesh. He combined the material's intrinsic qualities – hardness, coldness, impenetrability: symbols of the invincible woman – with the totally contrasting features of traditional supple fabrics – a fabric's ability to cling to the body, the possibility of draping it, its malleability when it is cut and sewn, and the way it can be dyed, patterned or appliquéd. Versace developed the material in collaboration with a German craftsman, reinterpreting the principle of interlinking rings in a metal mesh. In Versace's version, the rings do not interlink with each other, but serve to join a series of solid discs at four points. This construction of disks creates a smooth, even and highly flexible surface: Oroton.

Since 1982–83, Oroton has appeared in every collection. On each occasion, Versace would introduce slight modifications to the qualities of the material that were in-keeping with that season's ethos: from the soft drapery of the dresses of Spring/Summer 1984 to the neoclassical tunics of 1997; from the Klimt-inspired decorative details of Autumn/Winter 1985–86 to the diamanté-studded tunics of 1997–98. Plain or patterned, lacquered in rich, dark colours or in the pastel shades of more recent seasons, printed or studded with diamantés, or combined with leather, lace or the lightest of chiffons, Oroton has come to symbolize Versace's ability to reinvent an age-old material.

Using the Material

The second phase of the material's reinvention would begin when Versace decided to use the material in non-traditional ways, according to the same set of principles that had influenced him at the stage of intervening in the making of the fabric, namely transposition, role reversal, combining elements out of context and challenging the natural qualities of the material. His Oroton dress with a crinoline skirt illustrates the latter. By its nature, metal mesh is perceived as heavy and one would expect it to cling to the body; instead, it sits there, suspended and puffed up, as if it were the lightest of materials. In a similar way, he used a padded and quilted fabric, usually associated with weight and warmth, on a low-necked summer dress with a wide balloon skirt.

Versace enjoyed subverting the widely accepted features that distinguished male from female fashion. His transferring of elements from the woman's wardrobe into the male wardrobe is one of the most significant examples of Versace's reversal of sexual roles. The first of these elements to make the crossover was the silk shirt printed with a multicoloured pattern. We find it as early as Spring/Summer 1985 and it remained a constant feature of the collections up until the Miami shirt of 1993.

More daring, however, was the male version of draping. It appeared for the first time in the trousers of the Autumn/Winter 1983–84 menswear collection; Versace used the technique in a tweed fabric which, by its very nature, is not suited to draping. It reappears again as the leitmotif of the Autumn/Winter 1989–90 collection; here, it is applied to wool grisaille, a fabric which is so traditionally male and yet so naturally receptive to being draped into soft folds. In patterned fabrics too, the Versace man enjoyed decorative luxuries that had not been seen since the end of the eighteenth century. One example is a Jacquard woven wool with a spotted fur pattern of Autumn/Winter 1986–87 in which the grey hues are not quite sufficient to tone down the revolutionary message of the animal skin design.

However, it was with the waistcoat that Versace managed to recover some of the highly decorative elements that menswear lost with the French Revolution: colour, lace, pattern, embroidery. In the Autumn/Winter 1982–83 collection, a satin waistcoat embroidered to resemble an eighteenth-century waistcoat was glimpsed beneath a brown worsted dinner jacket. Eye-catching cherry-red and lemon-yellow waistcoats were edged with wide bands of openwork embroidery to accompany tailcoats in Autumn/Winter 1989–90. Finally, in 1996, silk waistcoats printed with the 'Wild Baroque' motif were then lavishly embroidered with gilt lamella spirals, studs and sequins.

The twentieth-century woman's wardrobe is crammed with fabrics that have been appropriated from the male repertoire, but Versace took things one stage further. He would borrow a fabric from the male wardrobe, but the style of the outfit he designed would then deny it its masculine qualities. For example, pin-stripe woollen skirts ended in enormous bows tied around the knees or developed layers of very feminine flounces in Autumn/Winter 1987–88, while the Prince of Wales check was padded, embroidered, or unpicked by hand and then transformed into a strapless evening dress.

Taking elements completely out of their historical and traditional context and then combining them is a constant feature of Versace's designs. As far back as his earliest collections, Versace adored daring combinations, such as leather and silk, suede and linen, metal mesh and woollen jersey, jute and gold, metal mesh and diamantés; he would harmonize these apparently dissonant combinations through his use of colour and proportion. In his final collections, on the contrary, he began accentuating the juxtaposition of materials through colour: purple leather and black lace, silver-coloured metal mesh and green python skin. Or he emphasized the disjunction by overdoing the finish: pleated and crumpled lamé silk voile combined with pleated patent leather. The sacrilegious nature of such combinations was a technical refinement of a tendency to violate which had already been seen in earlier years, when he expressed it by simply using a material or a colour totally out of context. A good example is the Spring/Summer 1986 bridal gown in black silk with bright red trimming.

Throughout his career, Versace constantly intervened in the production of his materials, though obviously his approach changed over the course of twenty years. He became increasingly confident with fabrics and introduced sophisticated amendments that gave him the desired custom-made textiles with which to design his collections. The first dresses in Oroton date back to Spring/Summer 1983 and the menswear and womenswear collections of 1983–84 already employed many of the methods for handling leather and embroidery that Versace would continue to use and refine throughout his career. And it was as early as the following winter that we find the first example of Versace intervening in a patterned fabric. The summer of 1986 marked the beginning of his keen interest in printing and finishing processes, which he saw as a means of achieving more dramatic textures than those that could be achieved by weaving. Starting in Autumn/Winter 1987–88, his imagination ran wild for a couple of years with printing to shape, a method of replacing and transposing the technique of embroidery. From 1994, he experimented with ever more daring and commercially risky finishes, such as coating and spraying garments with polyurethane.

His early reinventions required an enormous amount of courage given that they were totally cutting edge and against tradition – though they were conspicuous, they were technically far simpler than the experiments of later years. By the end of the 1980s, Versace's considerable success had given him the confidence to embark on two separate paths of research. On the one hand, he explored more complex materials: he was searching for a contemporary technical means of expression that would be able to convey the joy and pleasure that must have been felt when wearing and touching the lavish and costly clothes of the past. On the other hand, he continued to develop the dramatic showiness associated with the theatre costumes that brought him great acclaim. In some ways, Versace can be summed up by his relationship with the theatre, which is based on the ultimate role reversal: between the stage and everyday life. In his theatre costumes, we find skilfully embroidered ecru linen, pure silk grounds and appliqués of the highest quality diamantés. These are all materials which can only be appreciated close up, so are somewhat wasted on a theatre audience. In his designs for the catwalk, on the other hand, we find exaggerated shapes, appliqués of large stones and violent colour schemes more typical of theatre costumes, which need to be readily visible from a distance and in the dark. Versace used materials to give his designs a sense of dramatic sensationalism, that element of dream and illusion that belongs not to everyday life but to its representation.

It is along these two distinct but parallel paths that Versace's research into materials continued until 1997. He would disguise subtle novelty as a vulgarity that had been seen countless times before; the dress that looks as if it is made of cheap plastic as it would have been in the 1960s is, in fact, plastic-coated silk. He made printed kid look like golden reptile skin for a spring coat; it was scandalous from many points of view, but was luxurious to the touch. Versace enjoyed breaking rules and, like the best, most productive periods in the history of weaving, this meant making new, lively discoveries and pushing art and technology forward at a rapid pace. It has been claimed that in his work Versace consistently drew on tradition, but only to desecrate it and deny the past. In fact he had huge respect for and knowledge of the past which he united with a bold vision of the future – reasons why he could afford to be so daring and transgressive.

Woven Patterns

In figured fabrics the pattern is defined by the way the warp threads are interwoven with the weft threads. This technique dates back to the fourth millennium BC in China. The type of interlacing, known as the weave, often gives the fabric its name: plain weave, satin, velvet, and so on. In patterned weaves, the geometric pattern is created not only by the weave but by the use of different colours, by the twist of the threads, and sometimes by introducing different types of fibre (linen, wool, silk, etc.). Curvilinear patterns with subtle colour variations are achieved by using a combination of complex and different weaves in the same piece of material. Further decoration can be added by mechanical methods (fulling, watering, coating, etc.) or by heat processes, which alter the texture of the woven fabric.

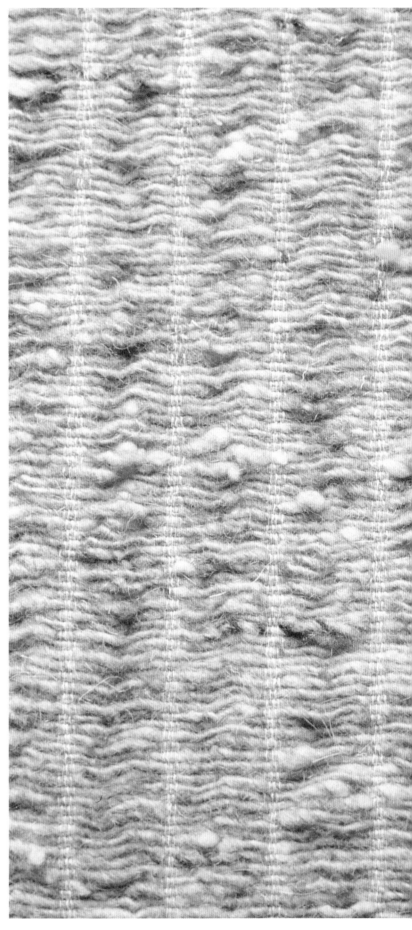

1

Woven Pattern
Autumn/Winter 1986–87
Double-faced Jacquard.
Lambswool, dyed in the hank.
Manifattura Loro Piana.
(opposite, far left)

On a grey worsted ground, the
black carded weft threads appear
much softer and in higher relief,
accentuating the spotted fur
effect. A pattern from the female
repertoire, with a closely set
double row of buttons, is
transformed into a man's suit in
the game of transposition of
which Versace was so fond.

2

Bands and Stripes
Autumn/Winter 1984–85
Double weave. Lambswool,
mohair, alpaca, dyed in the hank.
Manifattura Faliero Sarti.
(opposite, left)

A loosely twisted yarn of two
different colour threads is used in
a double weave in which the
unevenness and thickness of the
loose weft threads creates a gentle
stripe effect. The fabric is normally
associated with warm and figure-
hugging garments, but with
Versace's love for contradiction, he
used it for loose-fitting cabanes.

3

Bands and Stripes
Autumn/Winter 1983–84
Tweed. Lambswool, dyed in the
hank. Manifattura Faliero Sarti.
(left)

Since the eighteenth century,
tweed has been a coarse fabric,
characterized by different
coloured flecks and an uneven
surface. Here the inconsis-
tencies are exaggerated to create
wide, tonally contrasting stripes
in a fabric used for a formal
woman's ensemble.

4

High Tech
Autumn/Winter 1995–96
Patterned plain weave. Wool
(60% lambswool, 40% mohair)
and cellophane. Bleached in
the hank and finished with a
pearly polyurethane resin.
Manifattura Corisia (fabric)
and Memphis (finish).
(right)

A new take on Chanel's woollen
fabric, this version is covered in a
synthetic film, which destroys the
original material's characteristic
softness and three-dimensionality.
Once again, the classic prototype
has been denied some of its
inherent qualities.

5

High Tech
Autumn/Winter 1995–96
Loom-woven broken twill with
additional threads woven in by
hand. Wool (80% lambswool,
20% mohair), cotton chenille and
nylon trefoil. Bleached in the
hank. Manifattura Agnona (fabric)
and Vichi Ricami (hand-sewing).
(below left)

Coco Chanel took chenille from
eighteenth-century silks and
introduced it into her woollen
fabrics. Versace went one step
further and introduced a bright
synthetic fibre which adds
luminosity to the effect that has
been created by different
thicknesses of thread. The
mixture of precious wool and a
synthetic fibre is typical of
Versace's flair for combining
elements out of context. Although
the nylon is cheap, the fact that it
is woven by hand enhances the
value of the finished fabric.

6

High Tech
Autumn/Winter 1995–96
Silk and patent synthetic lamé.
Manifattura Fabric.
(below, right)

The type of synthetic yarn and the
weaving technique used here
remain a closely guarded secret.
The extreme expense and the
width of the fabric – a mere 70cm
– indicate that it was woven on a
hand loom, which is very rare in
this day and age, even in haute
couture. Once again, we find an
historical transposition: an ancient
weaving technique employed in
the production of a futuristic
fabric. Versace called the fabric
Nasa and used it for minimal
women's space outfits. As the
wearer moves, the surrounding
light sources are reflected in a
multitude of iridescent hues.

Printed Fabric

Textile printing involves the mechanical application of decoration to an already woven fabric. The technique had already reached outstanding levels of sophistication, especially in India, by the sixteenth century. The pattern is achieved by either adding colour (application) or by removing it (discharge). To add colour, the dye is either applied directly to the relevant areas or – having first applied resist to the areas that are not being coloured – the fabric is soaked in dye. To remove colour, an acid substance is applied to the dyed fabric. The subsequent chemical reaction either reveals the original colour or produces a synthetic colour that differs from the background hue. The technique involves using either engraved rollers (roller printing) or screens arranged in a geometrical shape (screen printing). As a new roller or screen is needed for each colour, screen printing, which is more difficult, is most worthwhile when producing a pattern in several colours and when the design motif is both large and complex.

7

Multicoloured Printing
Autumn/Winter 1989–90
Printed velvet hand-painted with gold pigment. Silk, dyed in the hank. Manifattura Redaelli (velvet) and Giuseppe Menta (application). *(below left)*

For the first season of the Atelier haute couture line, Versace chose the most sumptuous fabric ever produced – silk velvet. He decorated it with gold, not weaving it as had been done in the past, nor printing it as Fortuny had done, but hand-painting it. Rather than a traditional Renaissance, Baroque or Oriental motif, Versace chose a spotted pattern, which on the brown velvet pile produces a surreal and evocative effect. Having used historical features in a non-historical context, he further overstepped the mark by using the fabric for an Oriental sarong.

8

Multicoloured Printing
Spring/Summer 1991
Silk satin. Screen printing in eleven colours. Manifattura Ratti. *(below)*

A complex pattern with numerous colours and shades, in a large-scale design module (96 x 140cm) which requires accurate and costly printing, is used for evening dresses, as well as for shirts and dressing gowns for both men and women. An incredibly expensive fabric is used for appropriately expensive garments, but printed as though it were a T-shirt. In what appear to be just a few gaudy colours, we recognize the faces of legendary Hollywood figures, printed in the immortal 'Andy Warhol' style. (See Art 8, p. 87)

Designing with Discharge Printing

In both examples, the soft silk ground contrasts with the coarseness of the animal skin evoked by the pattern, with gold patches suggesting splashes of mud on the rhinoceros hide. From Spring 1983 onwards, Versace explored the theme of animal skin in a variety of textiles, from woven patterns to mixed techniques. He was always searching for new ways of evoking an animal hide without directly imitating it. It is a game of exchange: between woman and beast, between reality and imagination.

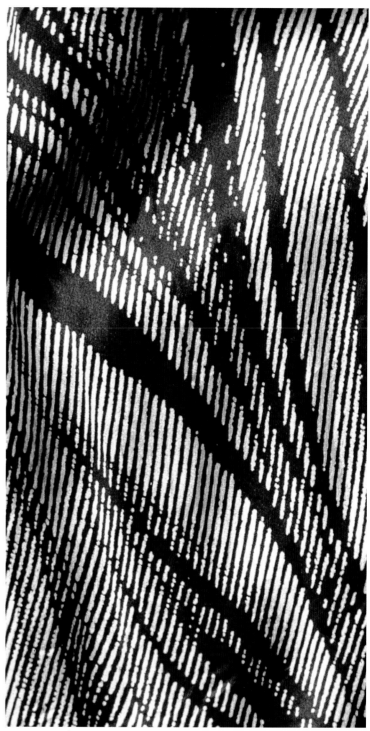

9

Designing with Discharge Printing
Spring/Summer 1986
Crêpon satin. Silk, dyed black and discharge-printed by hand.
Manifattura Giuseppe Menta.
(below)

Extremely advanced technology is applied to an ancient theme. The crêpe thread used in the weft forms a relief pattern that is then discharge-printed by hand. The concertina effect that is created when the wearer moves resembles the movement of animal fur and scales, introducing a striped version of the animal skin theme so often used by Versace.

10

Spring/Summer 1986
Satin, silk dyed black in the bolt, printed by discharge.
Manifattura Giovanni Canepa.
(above)

11

Spring/Summer 1986
Satin, silk dyed black in the bolt, printed by discharge and application of gold pigment.
Manifattura Giuseppe Menta.
(opposite)

Printing to Shape

The idea of weaving a pattern to shape was conceived in Lyon in the 1740s, and used on brocaded silks for men's tailcoats and waistcoats. The idea resurfaced around 1850 and was adapted for printing the flounces of the enormous skirts worn by women of that period. Versace took it up again and applied it to the printing of women's evening dresses, revisiting the theme of flounces, and to the printing of men's jacket and waistcoats (See History 17, p. 100 and The Ballgown 10, p. 67). Instead of disguising the body beneath, the flounces offer glimpses of it through full-length slits along the length of the leg, while the pattern on the waistcoat is more reminiscent of Balkan folklore than of Rococo decoration. Versace's inspiration can always be traced back to some historical precedent, but at least one of the elements is taken completely out of its usual context in his complex juxtapositions of references.

12

Spring/Summer 1989
Woman's vest. Printing to shape on linen cloth.
(opposite)

13

Spring/Summer 1989
Screen-printed linen cloth: one cloth. Manifattura TJSS.
(below)

Foulards

Printing to shape is the most widely used technique for the square patterns found in foulards. Just as he did with dresses, Versace broke with tradition when it came to foulards. However, he made continual references to the past through two strategies that lay at the heart of his creative genius: excess and out-of-context combinations. The gilt Baroque volute is an archetypal motif for a foulard pattern, but, when combined with black and white optical geometry or spotted animal skin, the effect can be provocative. With this in mind, decorating a foulard with the ultimate iconographic motif – a framed image of the Virgin Mary – appears almost blasphemous. Another example of mixing elements that have been taken out of their usual context was Versace's use of images of mass communication – postcards of exotic holiday destinations, such as Miami, or a portrait of the singer Elton John – which he transposed from a T-shirt on to expensive multicoloured screen-printed silk. Densely layered images, such as Baroque and Neo-Baroque theatre curtains, generally take over the entire ground of a foulard. Here, on the contrary, they are repeated four times, in rich, contrasting variations in a superfluity of colours and detail. As with the subject matter, the chromatic schemes are always contrasting or even clashing. An over-indulgence of colours intensifies the astonishing effect created by such bold combinations and decorative extravagance. In this vein, Canova's marble sculpture is presented in rich, dark shades of purple, black and orange. Versace's transposition of the printed-to-shape patterns of foulards to create dresses constitutes one of his most important innovations. The textile patterns obviously do not match up on the various parts of the dress and, as a result, precious material is wasted in a garment that seems to contradict all the rules of dressmaking.

14

Curtains
Autumn/Winter 1990–91
Screen-printed twill: 11 colours.
Manifattura Ratti.
(below)

15

Baroque
Spring/Summer 1992
Screen-printed twill: 8 colours.
Manifattura Ratti.
(See Print 4, p.29)
(opposite, above left)

16

Wild Baroque
Autumn/Winter 1992–93
Screen-printed twill and crêpe:
10 colours. Manifattura Ratti.
(See Showstoppers 2, p.20)
(opposite, above right)

17

Canova
Spring/Summer 1991
Screen-printed twill: 17 colours.
Manifattura Ratti.
(opposite, below)

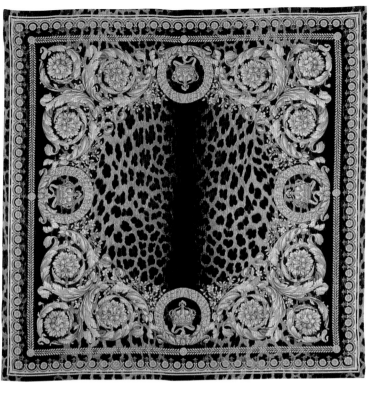

18

Autumn/Winter 1991–92
Man's dressing gown.
Screen-printed viscose velvet:
17 colours. Manifattura Ratti.
(left)

19

Icons
Autumn/Winter 1991–92
Screen-printed twill: 23 colours.
Manifattura Giuseppe Menta.
(See lining of History 13, p. 97)
(opposite, above)

20

Medusa
Spring/Summer 1992
Screen-printed twill:
13 colours. Manifattura Tria.
(opposite, below)

21

My Friend Elton
Spring/Summer 1991
Screen-printed twill: 15 colours.
Manifattura Tria.
(left)

22

Miami
Spring/Summer 1993
Screen-printed twill: 18 colours.
Manifattura Tria.
(left, below)

23

The Artist
Spring/Summer 1991
Screen-printed twill: 7 colours.
Manifattura Ratti.
(See Art 7, p.87)
(opposite)

Non-Woven Materials

Materials that are not made by interweaving threads and yarns are not fabrics. Animal hides were unquestionably the first form of non-woven material worn by prehistoric man. Then, with the invention of metal, clothing was created to protect the most vulnerable parts of the body. It was either cast in the shape of the area of the body that needed protecting, such as the suits of armour worn in late antiquity, or melted down to make the interlinking rings used in the mesh system, as in the medieval coat of mail. Ever since the first decades of the nineteenth century, when technology made it possible to produce thin sheets of rubber, this material has been used to make garments airtight and waterproof. In the twentieth century, and following the invention of synthetic materials, plastic was added to the list of non-woven materials.

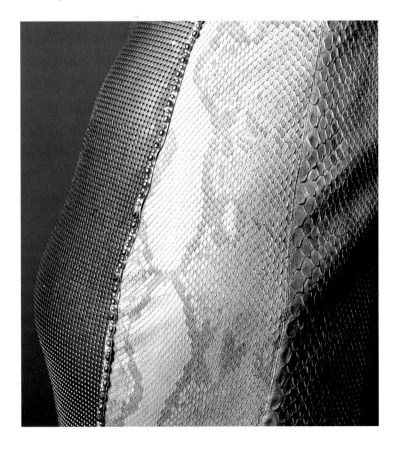

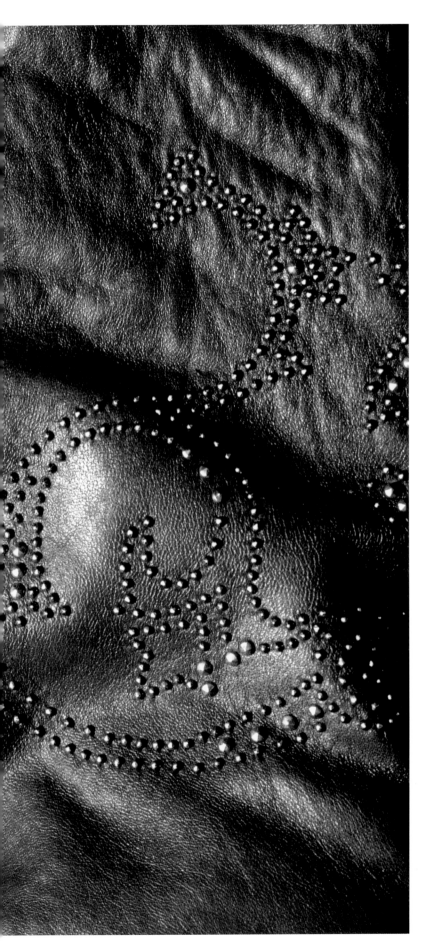

24

Non-Woven Fabric
Spring/Summer 1996
Metal mesh and leather.
Manifattura Modimex (metal
mesh) and Conceria (leather).
(opposite, far left)

25

Autumn/Winter 1988–89
Embroidered leather, leather,
cotton yarn. Manifattura Alfredo
Motta (leather) and Tonetti
(embroidery).
(opposite, left)

26

Autumn/Winter 1982–83
Leather with appliqué of metal
studs. Leather, white metal alloy.
Manifattura Alfredo Motta
(leather) and CIM Italia
(appliqué).
(left)

The two women's jackets
provide a subtle example of how
Versace transposed historical
genres. The studded leather of the
medieval warrior or the Middle-
Eastern prince is translated into a
lightweight woman's jacket worn
over floral-printed silk pantaloons,
while the delightful pale suede
embroidered with multicoloured
wool found in Nordic and
Hungarian folklore reappears
here in strictly black-on-black
geometric, vegetal motif
embroidery.

27

Animal Skin
Autumn/Winter 1986–87
Imprinted leather. Reversed
imprinted sheepskin.
Manifattura Alfredo Motta.
(below)

The inside-out sheepskin is
imprinted with a motif that brings
to mind the curly fleece on the
other side of the hide. Once again,
it is Versace's game of transposing
the natural characteristics of the
material, which he so often
played, even with printed and
patterned fabrics.

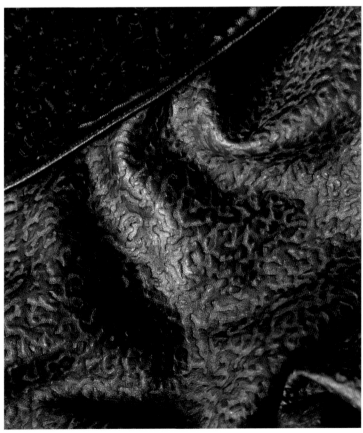

28

Animal Skin
Autumn/Winter 1992–93
Padded and quilted leather.
Manifattura Alfredo Motta.
(opposite)

Versace's padding of leather, in the
same way you would pad the softest
and lightest of fabrics, constitutes
an unusual use of materials. There
is further formal contradiction in the
use of the material to make a coat
with a tight-fitting bodice and
short flared skirt.

29

Animal Skin
Autumn/Winter 1989–90
Embroidered leather with
appliqué of metal studs. Leather,
cotton yarn, white metal alloy.
Manifattura Alfredo Motta
(leather) and Ruffo
(embroidery/appliqué).
(above right, right side)

30

Animal Skin
Autumn/Winter 1994–95
Crumpled leather. Aniline-treated
leather. Manifattura Alfredo Motta.
(above right, left side)

A labour-intensive and
complicated process is employed
here to make the leather look
crumpled and thus deny one of
the material's inherent qualities.
The result is a man's jacket which
hangs perfectly, as though it were
made from the best woollen
fabric. (See Leather 7, p.39)

31

Animal Skin
Autumn/Winter 1994–95
Imprinted and gilt leather.
Aniline-treated leather.
Manifattura Conceria.
(below, right)

The softness of the aniline-treated
leather is denied by the rigid,
reptile skin effect created by
the sophisticated imprinting
technique. The gilt finish removes
the material even further from
its original context.

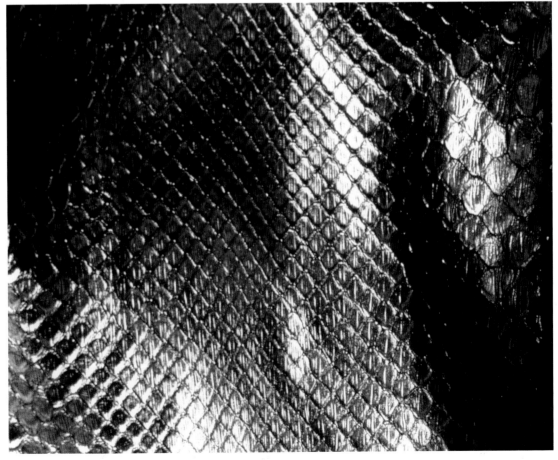

Metal Mesh

For his men's Autumn/Winter 1982-83 collection, Versace, drawing inspiration from the medieval warrior, presented leather corselets and jackets with inserts of mesh made from interlinking metal rings. The material proved to be unsuitable for womenswear and, just a few months later, together with a German craftsman, Versace developed Oroton. This is a mesh made of metal disks that contradicts all of the usual properties of metal: it clings to the body and can be draped, dyed or patterned.

The invention of Oroton constituted one of the most important advances in the field of postwar haute couture and, from 1986 onwards, Versace presented Oroton dresses in all of his collections. Sometimes he would use it by itself; at other times he created unlikely combinations with lace, animal skin, satin or chiffon. However, he always used Oroton for the type of slinky, close-fitting dresses that are usually made from soft, flowing fabrics. Defying sartorial tradition, Versace created the same effect with hard, heavy metal. (See The Ballgown 19-23)

32

Metal Mesh
Spring/Summer 1997
Metal mesh and lacquered
Oroton. Aluminium alloy.
Manifattura Modimex.
(opposite)

33

Metal Mesh
Autumn/Winter 1985–86
Black-resist lacquered Oroton,
with diamanté inserts. Brass
alloy. Manifattura Atelier
Friedrich Münch.
(above, left)

The gold hues of Klimt's
paintings are the inspiration
behind this season's collection.
The original concept adapts
very naturally to the metallic,
albeit extremely sensual material,
in one of Versace's most
successful translations of an
inspirational idea into a clothing
material. (See Art 1, p.83)

34

Metal Mesh
Spring/Summer 1985
Black lacquered and silver-
coloured Oroton with diamanté
inserts. Brass and aluminium
alloy. Manifattura Atelier
Friedrich Münch.
(below, left)

Oroton is made from four-pointed
stars which are interlocked by
fastening the points to very thin
rings arranged in a chequered
pattern. The right side of the
material resembles a sheet of
disks, while the reverse can either
be left exposed or used for
attaching diamantés or beads.

35

Metal Mesh
1987–97
Gold- and silver-coloured
or colour-lacquered Oroton.
Brass and aluminium alloy.
Manifattura Modimex and
Atelier Friedrich Münch.
(above, right)

The precious metal tones are
achieved by electrolysis, while the
other colours are sprayed on.

36

Rubber
Autumn/Winter 1983–84
Laser-patterned rubber.
Neoprene. Manifattura Cler-Prem.
(below, right)

Immediately after the medieval
knight and chain-mail look,
Versace proposed the man of the
future, dressed in rubber lined
with synthetic jersey. He designed
a jacket, trousers and even gloves
which keep the wearer extremely
warm. It is a brilliant example of
transposing a specialist material,
usually associated with protective
professional garments and
footwear, into everyday wear.
(See Leather 4, p. 36)

37

Plastic and Diamantés
Autumn/Winter 1995–96
Vinyl plastic with diamantés
and bead appliqués. Manifattura
Swarovski (diamantés) and
Vichi Ricami (appliqués).
(below, far right)

Precious Swarovski diamantés are
usually applied to expensive silk
grounds or to netting which they
completely cover. Here, they are
placed relatively far apart from
each other, to expose the lowly
non-textile material of the ground,
as well as the body beneath. It is
an audacious and almost
blasphemous combination of the
cheapest packaging material and
one of the ultimate symbols of
sumptuous clothing.

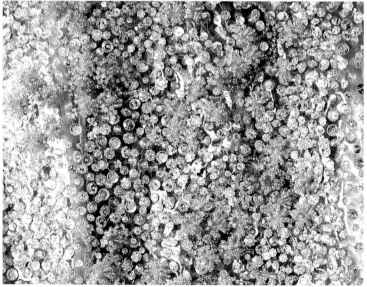

Mixed Techniques

Textiles are sometimes made by two or more overlapping or concurrent techniques. With embroidery, the oldest technique, a needle is used to trace a pattern on top of a textile support. The design of the pattern results from the repeated building up of threads of different types and colours. In earlier days, a needle and thread were used to sew non-textile materials on to a ground. At first, it was metal studs, corals, pearls and precious stones, but these were later replaced by diamantés and metal, crystal, glass or plastic beads, which now imitate the materials of the past. Embroidery has always yielded a highly desirable product, which could be reproduced on a technically and economically modest scale. Hand-embroidery is still practised across a range of different cultures and, over the course of several centuries, there have been no significant developments to the technique. Almost as ancient a technique is that of laying one fabric on top of another, with padding in between, and binding them into a single material through stitching. The technique was first used in Eastern countries that experience colder climates, and appeared in the West in the late Roman period. A more recent technique involves printing a pattern on a fabric that already has a woven pattern. This technique reached outstanding levels of sophistication in Japanese silks of the Edo period (1600-1868), but was not appreciated in the West until the end of the nineteenth century. In Edo fabrics, we also find complex mixtures of yarns and techniques that combine printing, embroidery and appliqués on different areas of the same piece of woven patterned fabric. Finally, in recent decades, we come across textiles that are the outcome of the mixing and/or overlapping of several different techniques, such as pattern weaving, printing, embroidery and appliqué. As well as being able to blend different fibres, there are also chemical, heat-based and manual finishing techniques that can be employed to alter radically and sometimes disguise the very nature of the fabric or fibre.

38

Embroidery by Appliqué
Spring/Summer 1996
Synthetic tulle with application
of leather, beads and sequins.
Manifattura Alfredo Motta
(leather) and Brambilla
(appliqués).
(See Leather 10, p. 41)

Embroidery by Appliqué I

Embroidery by appliqué using gold sequins dates back to the fifteenth century, and the technique of pulling out alternate warp and weft threads to create spaces to be decorated by either needle or bobbin appeared a century later. Versace drew inspiration from the ancient techniques employed to create sumptuous gold and polychrome curvilinear patterns, and then applied them to black and white optical patterns which are reminiscent of Escher's designs. Rigid and intrinsically well-defined materials are skilfully placed to create that confusion of focus which is normally associated with areas of subtle shading. The game of historical transposition and the reinvented use of old techniques is characteristic of Versace's designs.

39

Embroidery by Appliqué
Autumn/Winter 1986–87
Ground of hand-woven black
silk threads and appliqués of
glazed sequins. Manifattura
Vichi Ricami. (See The Ballgown
5 and 8, pp.64,66)
(right)

40

Embroidery by Appliqué
Autumn/Winter 1986–87
Voided ground with appliqués of
diamantés, sequins and
cylindrical metal and black plastic
beads. Manifattura Vichi Ricami.
(See The Ballgown 6, p.65)
(opposite)

Embroidery by Appliqué II

In 1989, Versace produced his first haute couture Atelier collection. For the occasion, he chose the opulent and showy technique – first used in Parisian ateliers towards the end of the nineteenth century – of covering the entire ground with appliqués. More appliqués were then applied to pieces of material on wire supports, which protruded three dimensionally as further embellishments. He fused formal and chromatic naturalism in homage to the aesthetics of Romanticism, which he then denied by putting the decoration on a corselet combined with a masculine trouser and tailcoat ensemble.

41

Autumn/Winter 1990–91
Appliqués of beads, cylindrical beads, sequins and diamantés on synthetic tulle. Manifattura Vichi Ricami. *(above, right)*

42

Spring/Summer 1989
Satin stitch embroidery in polychrome silk thread and appliqués of beads, diamantés and cylindrical beads on synthetic tulle. Manifattura Vichi Ricami. *(below, right)*

43

Embroidery by Appliqué
Spring/Summer 1992
Cotton and viscose faille printed in eleven colours and appliquéd with cloth flowers and gold beads. Manifattura Giuseppe Menta (fabric) and Vichi Ricami. *(opposite)*

Appliquéd cloth flowers in relief were widely used during the Rococo period and were a staple motif of female dress throughout the nineteenth century. However, they were rarely seen on a printed fabric and, on these rare occasions, were always used to accentuate a floral pattern. Versace, on the other hand, used a dense array of brightly coloured flowers to cover a pattern of inscriptions and futuristic motifs, a complete antithesis of the sumptuous arrangement of natural petals.

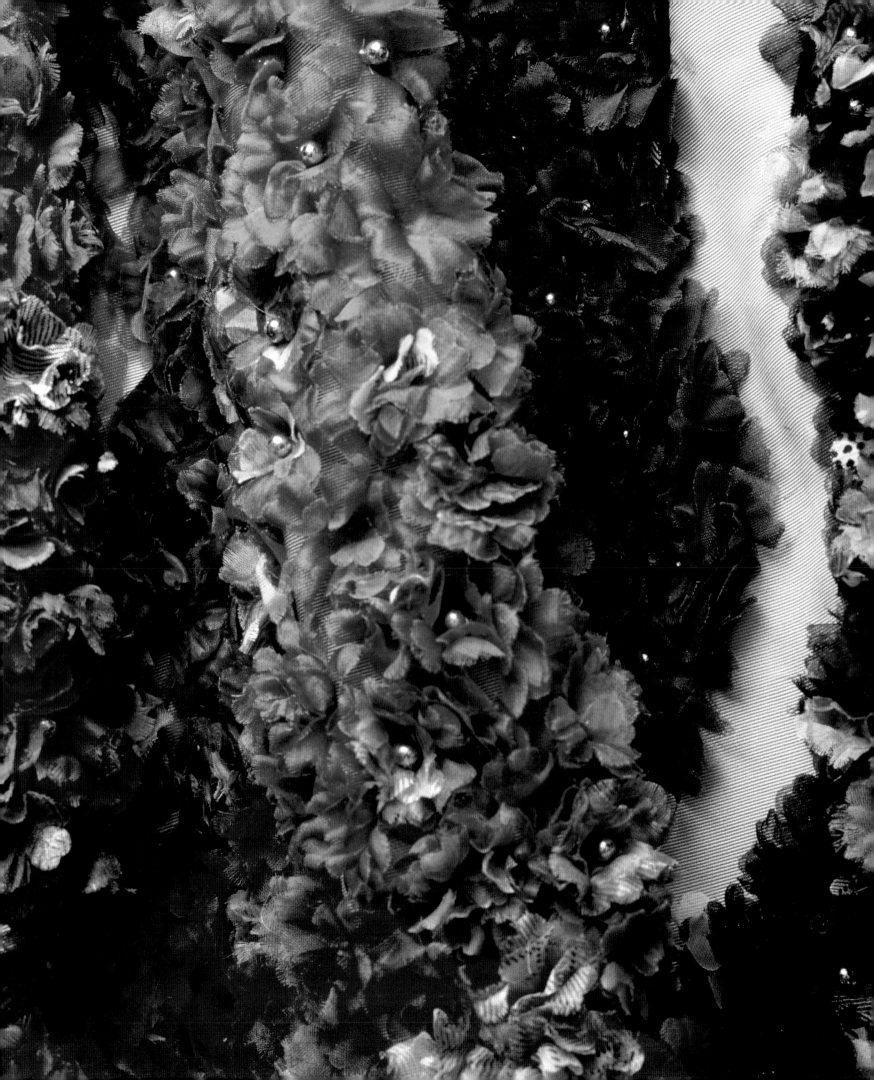

Embroidery by Appliqué III

The metal studs of a medieval warrior's rigid leather armour reappear as a gentle decorative effect on a feminine nineteenth-century redingote. The symbol of the cross embroidered with a cord and lamella spirals – found on the uniforms of high-ranking nineteenth-century military officers – is transposed from the crusader's cloak to the motorcycle jackets worn by the kind of women out to cause a scandal. The historical transposition of techniques, materials and garments is echoed in the reversal of masculine and feminine roles.

44

Autumn/Winter 1992–93
Leather with appliqués of metal studs. Manifattura Alfredo Motta (leather) and CIM Italia (appliqués). (See Daywear 14, p. 55)
(below)

45

Autumn/Winter 1991–92
Leather with appliqués of diamantés, beads, stones, braid and golden lamella spirals. Manifattura Alfredo Motta (leather) and Vichi Ricami. (See History 12, p. 97)
(right)

Free Associations I

Materials typically associated with rugged masculinity (leather and metal mesh for warfare and hunting) or those associated with professional, casual or domestic use (plastic) reappear as elegant women's dresses. Above all, they are treated like, and combined with, materials evoking the feminine qualities of softness, gentleness and delicacy: crêpe, lace, embroidered chiffon, pleated and silver lamé, voile.

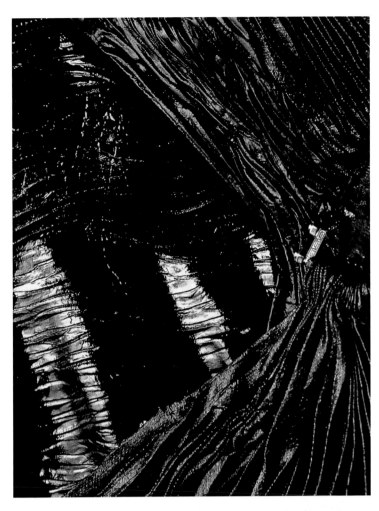

46

Autumn/Winter 1995–96
Woollen crêpe and vinyl.
Manifattura Teslan (fabric) and
Giovanni Crespi (vinyl).
(below)

48

Spring/Summer 1996
Brown lacquered Oroton,
silk chiffon and synthetic lace.
Manifattura Modimex (Oroton)
and Hurel (lace).
(below, right)

47

Autumn/Winter 1994–95
Patent leather, lurex lamé silk voile
and twill. Manifattura Alfredo
Motta (leather), Canepa (fabric)
and Omniapiega (pleating).
(above, right)

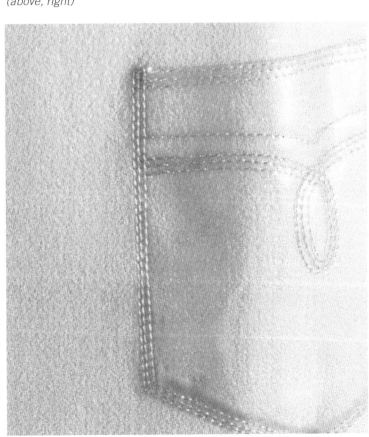

Free Associations II

Gold and silver lace, used for ceremonial court gowns and religious dress from the sixteenth to the end of the nineteenth century, were always combined with the most precious silk fabrics, very often embroidered in gold and silver. They were never used with printed fabrics, let alone with the decorative motif of animal skin. In the eighteenth century, spotted animal skin was highly prized for the exotic touch it gave to military uniforms.

It was very much later that it was introduced as either the main material or trim of women's coats. Never before had the spots of a leopard's skin been seen glittering with gold sequins. Throughout seventeen years of research and experimentation with contrasting combinations of historical and traditional elements, Versace always managed to bring a new dimension to his familiar repertoire of animal skin, embroidery and lace.

49

Spring/Summer 1992
Net of gold thread and beads applied to a 4-colour printed silk ottoman including gold pigment. Manifattura Luigi Verga (printing) and Vichi Ricami. (See The Ballgown 11, p. 68)
(below)

50

Autumn/Winter 1994–95
Printed plush with appliqués of gold sequins. Manifattura Franceschini (fabric) and Vichi Ricami.
(right)

Free Associations III

The Prince of Wales check appears regularly in Versace's stylistic repertoire. However, it never exists alone, as it does in the established tradition of British menswear fashions, and of womenswear in the second half of the twentieth century. For men, Versace gave it craquelé effects in 1987. A year later, for women, it was layered into a padded material and decorated with Baroque acanthus volutes, whose sinuous curves challenge the geometric precision of the underlying checks. In 1994, the shininess of polyurethane debased and, at the same time, embellished a woman's casualwear suit. In the most

recent collection, Versace's sister Donatella wanted to realize a technique that had first been adopted in 1994 by the Manifattura Crevacuore. Back then, cotton warp and weft threads were removed by a special finishing technique to create gaps, similar to those in openwork hems. When the technique was revived, the wefts were cut and pulled out by hand from the finished fabric to create small holes with irregular edges. The pulled-out threads were then secured by hand-stitching, in the ultimate violation of a fabric which, for a century and a half, had been rigidly defined by regular checks on a smooth and even surface.

51

Autumn/Winter 1988–89
Padded and embroidered Prince of Wales twill. Wool and cotton thread. Manifattura Loro Piana (fabric) and Zibetti (padding and machine embroidery).
(below, left)

52

Autumn/Winter 1994–95
Prince of Wales twill printed with iridescent polka dots. Wool and polyurethane. Manifattura Teslan (fabric) and Levati (finish).
(below, centre)

53

Spring/Summer 1998
Prince of Wales twill with cut wefts and warps. Wool. Manifattura Quaregna (fabric) and Ancilla Rigon (cut-work and embroidery).
(below, right)

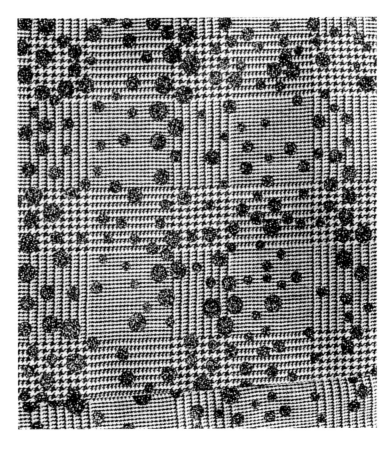
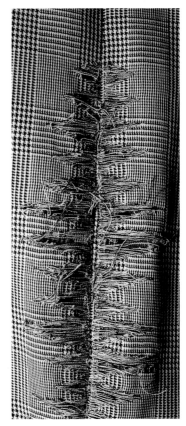

Crumpling

In the summer of 1986, Versace artificially and irreversibly crumpled a menswear outfit when he transposed grey pin-stripes to linen, depriving them of their usual aplomb. Eight years later, he revisited the concept of crumpling, this time applying it to velvets and satin, which, by their very nature, do not crumple as easily as linen. As in the case of the Prince of Wales check, he was completing a cycle of destructive manipulation and historical transposition.

54

Spring/Summer 1994
Wrinkled viscose velvet,
pleated silk satin and shot linen.
Manifattura Hurel (velvet),
Clerici (satin), Solbiati (linen)
and Omniapiega (finish).
(right)

High Tech

Lyon weavers in the mid-eighteenth century were masters of the art of treating a precious fabric in such a way as to understate its value, and of making a durable fabric weak and easily damageable. It was at a time when the wealth of the new bourgeoisie meant that they could afford any luxury, and aristocrats could only distinguish themselves by investing large amounts of money in fabrics that deliberately played down their wealth and, above all, would not last. Versace revived this strategy and applied it in drastic measure: by coating silk in polyurethane, he made it look like plastic. But the effect is only apparent, as the fabric retains its softness and warmth, its most notable qualities. It was the final act in Versace's mission to revive ancient techniques, carrying them to extremes, and it reflects his satisfaction at appearing to have a sacrilegious disregard of fabrics. Yet he loved precious materials too much to do without them and knew their characteristics too well to destroy them completely.

55

Autumn/Winter 1994–95
Silk taffeta coated with
polyurethane. Manifattura Vivatex
(fabric) and Limonta (finish).
(See Leather 8 and 9, p.41)
(left)

The Art and Craft of Gianni Versace

Claire Wilcox, Valerie Mendes and Chiara Buss

V&A Publications

Distributed by Harry N. Abrams, Inc., Publishers

First published by
V&A Publications, 2002
V&A Publications
160 Brompton Road
London SW3 1HW

Distributed in North America
by Harry N. Abrams, Incorporated, New York

ISBN 0-8109-6597-6 (Harry N. Abrams, Inc)

Library of Congress Control Number 2002102066

Front cover illustration:
Spring/Summer 1992, Linda Evangelista
© Irving Penn
Back cover illustration:
Photograph by Mark Harbeit
Illustrations featured on cover flaps:
front flap: pp. 95; 83; 101; 70; 92; 96;
back flap: pp. 29; 27; 81; 99; 111; 110
Title page illustrations: pp. 49; 56

Printed in Italy

Harry N. Abrams Inc.
100 Fifth Avenue
New York, N.Y. 10011
www.abramsbooks.com